DESIGNING WITH

GLASS

The Creative Touch

Carol Soucek King, Ph.D.

Foreword by Stanley Abercrombie, FAIA

Interior Details

AN IMPRINT OF
PBC INTERNATIONAL, INC.

Distributor to the book trade in the United States and Canada
Rizzoli International Publications Inc.
300 Park Avenue South
New York, NY 10010

Distributor to the art trade in the United States and Canada
PBC International, Inc.
One School Street
Glen Cove, NY 11542

Distributor throughout the rest of the world
Hearst Books International
1350 Avenue of the Americas
New York, NY 10019

Library of Congress Cataloging-in-Publication Data

King, Carol Soucek.
 Designing with glass : the creative touch / by Carol Soucek King.
      p. cm.
 Includes index.
  ISBN 0-86636-330-0 HB(dom.) (pb : 0-86636-439-0)
  1. Glass Construction. 2. Glass, Ornamental. 3. Glass art.
 4. Glass--Design. I. Title.
 NA4140.K46 1996   96-19758
 728--dc20   CIP

CAVEAT– Information in this text is believed accurate, and will pose no
problem for the student or casual reader. However, the author was often
constrained by information contained in signed release forms, information
that could have been in error or not included at all. Any misinformation
(or lack of information) is the result of failure in these attestations. The
author has done whatever is possible to insure accuracy.

—

Designed by Garrett Schuh

Color separation by Fine Arts Repro House Co., Ltd., Hong Kong
Printing and binding by C&C Joint Printing Co., (H.K.) Ltd., Hong Kong

10 9 8 7 6 5 4 3 2 1

Printed in Hong Kong

To Creativity at Home...
and Being at Home with Creativity!

CONTENTS

Foreword   6

Preface   8

Introduction   10

Luminous Pavilions   *12*

Nature Translucent   *48*

Urban Refractions   *86*

Classics Under Glass   *132*

Glossary   173

Directory   177

Index   182

Acknowledgments   184

FOREWORD

Sorry to repeat myself, but in the last sentence of a book titled *A Philosophy of Interior Design*, I wrote that interiors constitute "our most personal art." Carol Soucek King, I'm glad to see, seems to share the same view, for the admirable series of books Dr. King has planned promises to focus on just those aspects of interior design that make it personal.

The grand concept is not to be neglected, of course. Like any other art, interior design depends for its success on the encompassing vision that relates its many elements in a meaningful whole. But such vision, in interiors, becomes manifest and comprehensible through the medium of myriad details with which we are in intimate contact: the feel of a drawer-pull, the profile of a cornice, the polish and grain of wood, the "hand" of fabric.

This contact involves all our senses. We see our interiors, certainly, but we also smell the materials in them, we hear their acoustic properties, we brush up against their walls, step on their floors, open their casegoods, sit on their chairs. More than any other, interior design is the art we use. In that sense, it is not only our most personal art, but also the one most responsible for our well-being. In the context of increasingly brutalized urban environments, this is increasingly true and increasingly important. Interior design is often our refuge.

It is therefore a very welcome prospect that Dr. King is turning her experienced editorial eye to the details and materials on which the art of interior design depends. I'm sure we will all benefit from her discoveries.

~**Stanley Abercrombie**, FAIA
Chief Editor, INTERIOR DESIGN

PREFACE

To make the most of the design of our living environments, whether large or small, lavish or simple, is an opportunity too great to ignore, for it is a way of expressing who we really are and of elevating the function and spirit of our daily lives.

This is the third book in a four-volume series devoted to showing how various materials can be used to shape both space and mood through bringing color, light, texture and definition to our homes. DESIGNING WITH GLASS: *The Creative Touch* focuses on this magnificent translucent substance and its radically expanding design potential as an architectural as well as a traditional decorative tool and transmitter of light.

I feel extremely fortunate to have been able to reflect the creativity of some of the world's outstanding architects, interior designers and artists through their myriad uses for glass and its endless variety of forms. They bevel, etch, sandblast, mold, sculpt and paint it. They order it in blocks and panes, tinted and reinforced. They dissolve boundaries between outdoors and interiors, emphasize the oneness of light and space, refract light into closed urban spaces and extend our vision into landscapes unbounded. On the following pages, they unfold the enabling functionalism, the enlivening brilliance and empowering beauty that can be achieved in our living environments through the use of this lustrous and inspiring medium.

~**Carol Soucek King**, *Ph.D.*

INTRODUCTION

The utility of glass has been recognized and valued since the beginning of recorded history. The first glass was of volcanic origin and was probably more translucent than transparent, but its versatility made it a prized commodity. History is unclear as to whether the Egyptians or Phoenicians were the first to make glass, but the Romans were the first to manufacture glass commercially.

The dawn of the Renaissance found glass being commonly used to glaze windows in buildings. While its primary functions were to let light in and keep cold out, there was sufficient heat gain through the glass openings to make dwelling spaces with openings preferable to those without and thus glass, with its durability and multiple uses, was permanently established as a product of commerce.

For most of history, sheet glass, characterized by uneven surfaces, varying thicknesses and visual distortions, was the only product available for glazing structures. In 1870, plate glass was produced commercially for the first time in this country. Plate glass was made by casting a blank or ribbon of glass and then laboriously grinding and polishing both surfaces until they were parallel. The parallel surfaces eliminated the visual distortion associated with sheet glass and provided a clear, unobstructed view of the outside.

Prior to electrical lighting, sheet glass was used extensively in skylights, clerestories and windows as a means of illumination and, to some degree, heating in industrial buildings, warehouses and other facilities with large, open work areas. Glass, by letting the daylight in, served to remove some of the dreariness associated with these types of construction, thereby improving productivity. During this period, windows grew in size and number in most residential construction, and con-

sumers began to develop an awareness of the physiological and psychological contribution that glass makes to their lives by bringing the outside in. Research has demonstrated that light can have a healing effect on both the mind and the body.

In the late fifties and early sixties, float glass was introduced in the United States and quickly replaced plate and sheet glass as the principal product of the industry. The float process produced glass with parallel surfaces by floating the glass ribbon on a molten bed of metal. Float glass had excellent visual qualities and was much cheaper to produce than plate glass. Consequently, it rapidly replaced both plate and sheet glass, with the exception of some special applications requiring very thin glass that could only be made by the sheet process. A few years later, reflective glass was introduced, and the industry had its first product with a degree of design and performance flexibility innovative enough to move glass to the next plateau in its commercial development. Due to the soft coatings used, insulating glass units had to be made with reflective glass to protect the coated surface. While insulating glass was in its infancy, reflective glass, coupled with the energy crisis of the early sixties, dramatically increased the use of insulating glass units in residential and commercial construction overnight.

Simultaneously with the energy crisis, interest in safety glazing reached an all-time high. In the United States, for example, the Consumer Product Safety Commission adopted a uniform safety glazing standard requiring safety glazing materials to be used in hazardous locations (patio door units, tub and shower enclosures, storm doors and glazed panels immediately adjacent to entrance and exit doors). The so-called safety crisis significantly increased the use of tempered and laminated glass, two products that had been little used prior to safety regulations. While float, reflective, tempered and laminated glass provided the industry with a whole new repertoire of products for the times, manufacturing innovations of the last ten years have produced products so much more sophisticated than those of the sixties that comparisons are meaningless.

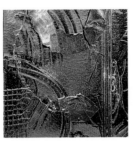

As DESIGNING WITH GLASS: *The Creative Touch* suggests, there are very few applications in today's market for plain vanilla glass. The needs are much more complex, with safety, sound reduction, security, energy conservation and resistance to hurricane winds being just some of the applications that glass is regularly asked to address. The product's versatility is unquestioned — it provides a constantly changing mural by bringing the outdoors in, it is used to create the feeling of spaciousness or intimacy, its colors cover the rainbow and range from vivid to muted, it can be transparent or opaque and can keep heat and light in or out. You have only to look to the glass in your own home, vehicles, appliances or office to appreciate its flexibility and impact on our daily lives.

In your own home, ordinary annealed glass is silvered to make your mirrors; it may also be tempered, depending on where and how it is used. Tempered, laminated and insulating glass are the products most likely to be used in your patio door unit, tub and shower enclosures, windows, skylights, clerestories, sun room, entrance and exit doors and windows or glass panels that are next to entrance and exit doors or are less than eighteen inches from the floor. In all probability, the insulating glass contains solar-reflective

or Low-Emissivity (Low-E) coated glass and the air space has been filled with heavy gas such as argon to substantially improve its insulating value.

Tempered glass has very likely been used in the control panels and windows of your stove and microwave and in the shelving of your refrigerator. Your hot tub, sauna, whirlpool and steam room must be safety glazed, and use either tempered or laminated glass. However, its extensive use in residential construction notwithstanding, architectural glass is not a do-it-yourself type of product. It requires expertise and careful handling and its installation should be left to experienced glaziers who are also knowledgeable about the requirements of the local building and fire codes.

In your car, you are literally surrounded by glass, laminated in your windshield and tempered in both your side and back lights. In the near future, it is anticipated that even more glass will be used in cars. The new glass is expected to convert the sun's heat into usable energy for use in running such things as the air conditioner.

While glass is used extensively in the workplace, these applications are little more than extensions of those found in the home. Typically, glass usage in the office includes partitions, shelving and, as a protective device for floors, desk tops and other surfaces. Even electrochromic glass, which causes metallic coated clear glass to become opaque when an electrical charge is applied, could be considered for residential use. Just imagine, a glass that by the flip of a switch can make your patio door unit opaque, thereby eliminating the need for expensive drapes. The development of

technology to make complex bends with glass has brought a new dimension to office design and many of these innovations will be translated to residential uses in the near future.

No other building material enjoys the versatility of glass. It can be transparent or translucent, it can be clear, tinted, colored or opaque, it can be used in combination with other materials to significantly enhance its energy, safety, sound-reduction and wind-resistance performance. At the same time it is extremely strong, durable, easy to maintain and affordable. Dr. King's illustrations effectively demonstrate that as a building material, glass is truly magical in its ability to provide pleasure and comfort in your home.

~William J. Birch
President, Association Services Corporation
Executive Vice President, Glass Association of North America
Administrator, Primary Glass Manufacturers Council
Adminstrator, Glazing Industry Code Committee

LUMINOUS
PAVILIONS

Hugh Newell Jacobsen &
Thérèse Baron Gurney

Ron Goldman

Edward R. Niles

Juan Montoya

Joan Gray & Anne Leepson

Dennis Jenkins Associates

Bart Prince

Gary Whitfield

W. Douglas Breidenbach

Meryl Hare & David Walker

FLEMISH PERSPECTIVES

Tempered Glass

Every view offered by this site in Holland, an overgrown and romantic nineteenth-century garden surrounding a quiet pond, is unique. Architect **Hugh Newell Jacobsen** used large expanses of glass to take maximum advantage of uncluttered vistas and which, on the gable ends, are deliberately glazed with muntin windows in the style of sixteenth-century architecture.

"The reflective surface defining interior spaces is the true aesthetic beauty of glass," says Jacobsen. "Glass is never a void, but when the surface, taut and shining, is used as a design aesthetic as well as a spatial definer, the result is clear and within the architectural order."

Interior designer for the project was Jacobsen's associate, **Thérèse Baron Gurney**, ASID.

GENERAL CONTRACTOR: *Project Team Alphen aan den rijn B.V.*

RIGHT *The design abstracts and accents the stepped gable ends of neighboring Dutch villages' sixteenth- and seventeenth-century houses. Because of the relatively low level of sunshine, the fenestration is clear beneath the eaves and mullioned on the stepped gabled ends where the windows reach for the light.*

Photography by Robert C. Lautman

The totally skylit center hall is capped at both ends with nearly identical stepped gable brick pavilions.

The dining room ceiling rises to twenty-two feet, half of it a skylight revealing the twenty-four-inch-diameter beech tree beyond.

LEFT & FAR LEFT *Mullioned windows, an all-glass bay for the kitchen breakfast area and a glass roof make the kitchen a pavilion of light and shadows. The bay is flanked by a pair of sliding glass doors.*

BELOW *Pure white paint, chosen for the exterior to emphasize the structure, is carried throughout the interior to emphasize and reflect the light.*

ABOVE *A brushed stainless steel stair with teak treads and glass handrail maintains the entry's axis.*

A SENSE OF PLACE

Tinted and Clear Tempered Glass &
Polymer-Dispersed Liquid Crystal

Two elements always play a prominent part in the architecture of **Ron Goldman** — the layering of interior spaces and the dissolution of distinctions between interior and exterior. For both he relies on an extensive use of glass, and perhaps no house could express that better than the home he designed for his own family in Malibu, California.

Large picture windows alternate with small ones to provide what he calls "post-card vignettes." The sense of entry is cele-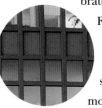brated inside and out by French doors with glass either clear or opaque. An extensive fiberglass skylight extending over most of the house provides a constant change of environment and light. Variously textured glass in both horizontal and vertical surfaces turns functional items into artful compositions. Finally, to continue the use of glass in the master bath yet provide privacy as well, glass tiles have been

TRANSLUCENT SKYLIGHTS: *manufactured by Kalwall, supplied and installed by Carmel Architectural Sales*
PLATE GLASS: **Libbey-Owens-Ford**
TEMPERING AND INSULATING UNITS: **A.C.I. Distributing**
POLYMER-DISPERSED LIQUID CRYSTAL: *previously manufactured by Taliq Industries, currently being manufactured by Polytronix, Inc.*
ALUMINUM CHANNEL: **U.S. Aluminum Corporation**
OPERABLE WINDOWS: **Metal Window Corp.**
INSTALLATION OF ALL GLASS: **Malibu Glass & Mirror/Gerald Lemonnier**

The three-story skylit space allows
all levels of the house to interact.

Photography by Undine Prohl

A shower pavilion between master bath and bedroom is made of glass tiles polished and back-painted blue to pick up the hues of ocean and sky.

Photography by Claudio Santini

painted and sandblasted, and polymer-dispersed liquid crystal turns one glass wall
from clear to opaque at the flip of a switch.
All support Goldman's continuing belief
that enclosures need not feel confining, but
instead, to the greatest extent possible,
should express an inseparable oneness with
the natural environment beyond.

On the small, 40-by-80 foot site, the design depends on the layering and contrast of walls and materials in a sequence of indoor and outdoor spaces, which are visually expanded by continuous sandstone flooring.

Photography by Undine Prohl

SYNTHESIZING TECHNOLOGY AND FORM

Tinted, Solar-Reflective Glass & Glass Block

Edward R. Niles believes in shedding all preconceptions about architecture and its established styles. More interested in the future than in the past, he tries to expose clients' attitudes, not their preconceived tastes. Believing residential architecture to be more "religious" than a church because of its ability to express and influence people's lives on a daily basis, he asks them about their values, not their desire for objects and glitz, and then makes these the imprints for their future homes.

Emotionally bounded by the future and the extension into the unknown, Niles does not feel that to be successful art has to be functional: "Some things can be made and not have a function other than being very pleasing to look at," he says.

Yet his unusual designs do have to function and they do have to be built, and every assemblage requires a tremendous amount of knowledge. Since Niles is not mass-producing but instead creating almost other-

STRUCTURAL ENGINEER: *Dimitry Vergun*
MECHANICAL ENGINEER: *American Energy Consultants*
GENERAL CONTRACTOR: *Edward R. Niles and Lisa Niles McCarthy*
SINGLE-GLAZED, GRAY-TINTED SOLAR-REFLECTIVE GLASS AND LAMINATED
GLASS: *Pittsburgh Corning Corp.*
GLASS INSTALLATION: *Dee's Glass*
TRANSLUCENT PANELS: *Manufactured by Kalwall, supplied and installed by Carmel Architectural Sales*

On a mountain site overlooking the Pacific Ocean, two acres of trees and variable topography provided an undisturbed natural setting for this residence, the concept of which was evolved over a five-year period by Edward R. Niles and architect **Lisa Niles McCarthy**. Finally the search for a synthesis of technology and form separate from the organic argument of the natural setting led to a discussion of an alien object, three-dimensionally observed and understood from the land but free from the predictable associations with Mother Earth. There is, by intention, a decided change in the form of the earth-connected object versus the disengaged "space station." The associated imagery of each forms the basis for constant argument and exploration.

The spaceship metaphor required that mechanical, electrical and structural systems be self-sufficient and self-contained. It was these systems — water source heat pumps, solar collectors, fan blowers and satellite receiver — that provided the genesis of the final architectural expression of an independent exploratory vehicle.

As specified in the State of California energy code (Title 24), the architects were required to perform an energy consumption analysis. The house is solar heated, conserving enough energy to allow the use of single glazing or laminated glass instead of double plates of glass.

Photography by Alan Weintraub

worldly structures, communicating the process to builders through the process of construction becomes an art in itself.

In the end, his clients have the good fortune to realize the future is just as important as the past and that, when addressed with knowledge and unbounded creativity, reaching for it can be a thrilling experience today.

The program was traditional in its basic needs — living, kitchen and dining rooms, which are located in the fan-shaped structure (pages 24-29), and master bedroom suite, office, laundry, exercise room and guest room, which are located in the long horizontal structure (page 24, top right). These two structures are connected by a glass-enclosed bridge (page 24, bottom). The clients' primary concern was the site, the views and a constant visual and physical contact with the natural surroundings.

The arched pavilion of translucent fiberglass and glass is an attempt to "land" the "space station," its connection with earth, the pavilion, by necessity a transparent, skeletal assemblage providing views of Planet Earth with the least obstruction. The structural system is a rigid frame, truss and box girder designed for hundred-mile-per-hour winds and maximum seismic acceleration. Materials include steel, concrete, fiberglass-insulated panels and stainless steel panels as well as glass.

A GLOWING SPACIOUSNESS

Tempered, Etched & Sandblasted Glass

To create a sense of greater space, **Juan Montoya** gutted and completely redesigned his client's home in Hewlett Harbour, New York, combining many smaller rooms into a few large ones that seem even more spacious due to the designer's use of tempered, sandblasted and etched glass.

ETCHED GLASS PANELS IN MASTER BATHROOM: **John Depp**

LEFT & ABOVE *In the living room, Juan Montoya transformed the idea of skyscraper buildings into a lamp composed of stacking disks and cylinders of sandblasted glass. Its strong sculptural quality visually extends the room's sense of height.*

OPPOSITE *Inspired by Art Deco motifs, Juan Montoya designed these glass panels for the master bathroom. Their transparency permits natural light to enter the enclosed space and define the delicate etched pattern, while still allowing for privacy within.*

Photography by Billy Cunningham

FOOTPRINT IN THE SAND

Tinted and Clear Tempered Glass

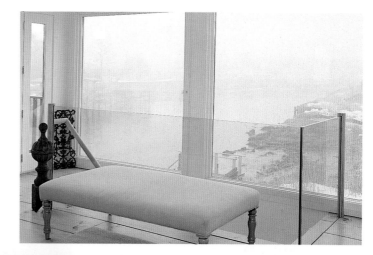

At Pat Robinson's Connecticut beachfront cottage, it is almost impossible to tell where the outside ends and the inside begins.

To keep the project to a renovation, as required by the strict local building code regulating waterfront properties, interior designer **Joan Gray** and builder **Anne Leepson** retained the original foundation and one old crooked wall. Otherwise, they completely replaced the ramshackle home and its dark, dreary little rooms with one open area upstairs for kitchen/dining/living and two downstairs for the bedrooms. Each is defined by walls of glass and hues of sand and sea, and everywhere the mood is as harmoniously settled as the driftwood along the salt marsh and river beyond.

TEMPERED GLASS AT WINDOWS: *Marvin Windows*
GLASS RAILING AND SANDBLASTED GLASS COUNTER: *Dimensions in Glass*

ABOVE RIGHT *So as not to obstruct the view yet conform to the Connecticut code requiring three-foot stair railings, the designers had one fabricated out of glass.*

RIGHT *The addition of a seventeenth-century door begins a running motif throughout of an old fishing cottage, while the ascent of the floating staircase past and toward large expanses of window commences the open, airy and contemporary feeling which predominates throughout.*

ABOVE *A series of single casement windows emphasizes vertical lines and also opens up to the deck.*

FAR LEFT *On the wall opposite the tub in the master suite, the headboard of the queen-size bed is an antique French mirror which further reflects the view.*

LEFT *Across from the sliding glass doors in the master suite is a mirrored wall which hides the toilet alcove. A cast-aluminum bowl, set into a thick slab of sandblasted glass topping a cabinet, serves as the sink. The faucet is set into the mirror itself.*

Photography by Alec Hamer

By raising the roofline the designers allowed for cathedral ceilings and a series of huge custom-made windows.

WATERSCAPE

Sandblasted & Airbrushed Glass

Its seaside location inspired a crystallized
water motif in the dining area of this
South Florida residence, for which **Dennis
Jenkins** and his associates **Kim Rizio** and
Laura Barrett designed every
space, wall and piece of furniture. Indeed, it would be dif-
ficult to imagine a more liquid experience unless one
were actually under water.

GLASS: *SGO Glassworks*
AIRBRUSHING: *Bischoff Studios*

*A combination of sandblasted and
airbrushed glass was used to turn a
dining table, buffet and sliding
glass doors into interpretations of
the sea beyond.*

*Photography courtesy of
Dennis Jenkins*

SEASIDE SCULPTURE

Solar & Stained Glass

The architecture of this coastal home designed by **Bart Prince** serves as a sculptural biography of the way its residents live. Built around a central courtyard and swimming pool, a sequence of spaces leads from the street to the dwelling's most private parts, a sequence reflecting each family member's individual needs.

Truly designed from the inside out, the home seems like one giant undulating seashell, protected from the world by a solid glue-laminated shingle-covered roof. Three copper-covered geometric structures cantilevered from the ground step their way to the ocean through pool and courtyard, with the more private areas in the higher structure and the main living areas in the two below. Amid this expansive use of wood and the sense of enclosure it provides, the architect's use of solar and stained glass for light, color and visual access to the ocean below seems like a king's ransom in jewels but far more essential.

LEFT *At the courtyard in the center of the house, a large circular window opens into a two-story interior space. The glazed sections of the window project toward the pool area, giving the window a three-dimensional quality.*

BELOW *Solar gray glass projects beyond the supports outside the master bedroom and Japanese bath, thus allowing a person inside to lean into the window to look down the beach below.*

RIGHT *The glass sections are designed not as a flat plane but rather as projecting panels.*

Photography by Alan Weintraub

TOTAL INTEGRATION

Tempered, Frosted & Tinted, Solar-Reflective Glass

An innovative plan that makes myriad connections between interior and exterior creates a great sense of openness in the Jeff and Hannah Kirschner residence in Santa Monica, California. Considering its narrow, undistinguished, mid-block location and the need to surround it with walls for privacy, the achievement is notable.

"The challenge was to create a special residence from a very ordinary setting," says architect **W. Douglas Breidenbach**, whose first decision was to put the garage at a subterranean level so that he could open up the entire first level, both interior and exterior, for living space. Both side yards became integral parts of the plan, and a reflecting pool that is built above a lower-level side-yard passage extends the usable space to the lot's entire width.

The decision to place the garage underground enabled the entry to be placed at the structures' side and to be approached through an uncluttered naturescape. A frosted, mullioned glass door leads to a courtyard which takes visitors past the guest room and to the glass entry door. Immediately inside, a two-story space bisects the home's living and dining areas and fills

ABOVE & RIGHT *A descending driveway at left takes cars underground, eliminating from view the ever-present garage and enabling the approach to the Kirschner residence's side entry to be a nature walk.*

Photography by Douglas Hill

them with an abundance of natural illumination pouring in through a cruciform-
shaped skylight overhead. The shape of the
skylight reflects the plan's two axes, thus
defining the home's four quadrants with
light. With the exterior walls' glass detailing
erasing all feeling of division from the rear
and side gardens, the entire space exudes a
feeling of light and expansiveness that, for
such a narrow site, is extraordinary.

FIXED WINDOWS: *custom fabricated by Morrow & Morrow Corporation*
SKYLIGHT: *J & M Manufacturing*
OPERABLE WINDOWS: *Design Supply*

ABOVE LEFT *The cruciform skylight
is tinted so that, while it lets in an
abundance of light, it eliminates
heat gain almost entirely.*

ABOVE RIGHT *Ample fenestration
enables light to pour into all living
areas, making them feel at one with
the garden beyond.*

RIGHT *Frameless glass doors open to
a reflecting pool, further minimiz-
ing the separation between interior
and exterior.*

LIGHT SOURCE, SUN SHIELD

Glass Block, Tempered Glass & Tinted, Solar-Reflective Glass

Located on Middle Harbour in Sydney, Australia, this home was partially remodeled by architect **David Walker** and redesigned by interior designer **Meryl Hare**, both working to take advantage of the inspiring view and welcome inside lavish doses of northerly light.

"The clients' brief was to make the home more reflective of their natural, laid-back harborside lifestyle yet suitable for entertaining friends and business associates," says Hare. "In addition, the decor needed to take cognizance of the modern finishes of the house, such as the stainless steel, granite, high-gloss polyurethane and glass, yet the clients wanted the overall effect to be soft and comfortable as well."

In supplying all new furnishings for the house, which commenced long before the architectural remodeling, Hare replaced the original flooring and carpets with timber strip flooring of Tasmanian Oak and the

ABOVE RIGHT *The protective awning, while not impeding the view, softens the interior and protects fabrics from sun damage.*

RIGHT *A conservatory style window extends the study and links it with the lush tropical garden. This addition was designed by David Walker to further maximize light into this back area of the home.*

Photography by Richard Waugh

The entire view is exposed with glazing. However, as a shield against sun damage and to provide weather shelter, a sun awning was constructed using eighty-five percent ultraviolet tinted glazing supported by aluminum trusses.

carpeted stairs with black Sydney Granite to marry with existing granite in the entrance. All other carpets were replaced with natural sisal. She achieved the desired soft, comfortable feeling through cottons and silks in the harbor's colors of blue, green, cream and lilac — delicately hued fabrics that made it especially important that the additions of glass not compromise the interior with damaging ultraviolet rays. The architectural additions, which included an extra glass-walled bedroom level, a curved wall of glass block between dining and kitchen areas and vast glazing to expose the view, used sun shields and tinted, solar-reflective glass extensively for protection.

ABOVE *Glass blocks were also incorporated into the dining room to bring light into an otherwise dark area.*

RIGHT *The main bathroom is located within the master bedroom and open to it via a double-glazed wall that lightens the bedroom from both east and west. Adjustable venetian blinds afford privacy.*

TINTED, SOLAR-REFLECTIVE GLASS AND TEMPERED GLASS: *Skydome Pty Ltd.*
GLASS BLOCK: **Dunstone Maze Pty Ltd.**

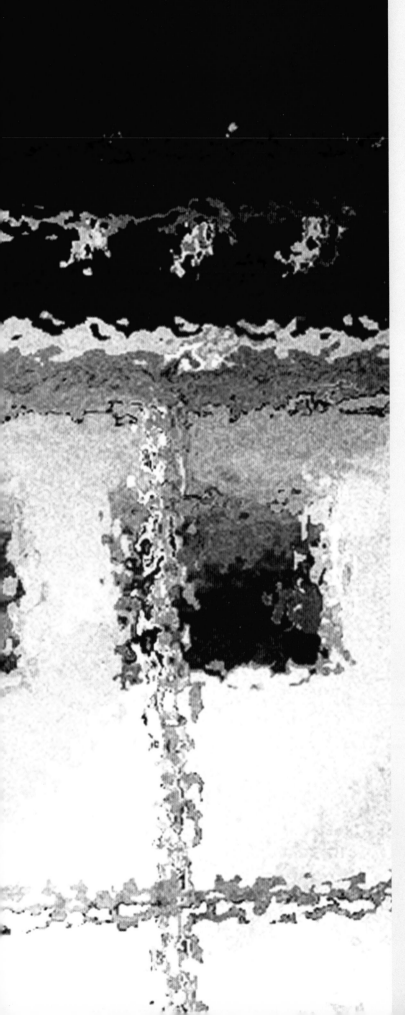

NATURE
TRANSLUCENT

Kari Kuosma Architects

Alfredo De Vido

Angelo Tartaglia

Perry Janke

Franco Audrito &
Christopher Rebman

Robert Whitfield &
Louis Shuster

Peter Forbes & Associates &
Christine Maclin

James P. Wright

W. Douglas Breidenbach

Buff, Smith & Hensman &
Sheri Schlesinger

Agustin Hernandez

James Blakeley III

IDEAS FOR A NEW MILLENNIUM

Tempered Glass, Glass Block & Acrylic

It came as no surprise to see a social and environmental awareness expressed in this experimental house for an exhibition in Malmö, Sweden. A consciousness regarding what is good for the public and the planet has often marked contemporary Nordic design. So the aim of this award-winning design by **Kari Kalevi Kuosma** and **Esko Valkama** directed toward the need for better low-cost, space-efficient urban dwellings could have been expected. Yet no one could have predicted the extent of their solution's creativity.

For these Finnish architects, a concern for self-expression and privacy in a world of decreasing individual space was of major significance. Each activity, such as cooking, sleeping and reading, was assigned its own special area and given its own special character through color, shape and material to an extraordinary degree. From jubilant entries to airy areas on top for gardening and sunning, spirited accents of paint, ceramic tile, acrylic and glass complement

Geometric elements in brilliant colors reminiscent of early-twentieth-century Russian avant-garde art lend a deconstructivist appearance, expressing the architects' intention to provide the building blocks for future houses in which every segment can be taken apart, rethought and rearranged for each individual's needs.

GLASS, GLASS BLOCK AND ACRYLIC: *Lohja/Uniplast/Finland, through* **Keraplastoy**

As the limited size could have felt too confined, the architects decided to make the home as transparent as possible, using glass, glass block and perforated acrylic for skylights, windows and walls of various dimensions to bring light deep within and augment the sense of spaciousness.

The upper floor contains a greenhouse and terrace. The hallways, which can be covered with a curtain, usually are open to the sky.

Photography by Jussi Tianen

INSIDE/OUTSIDE UNITY

Plate Glass

The overall design intent of architect *Alfredo De Vido* is for each of the homes he creates to relate to its natural surroundings to the greatest extent possible. In realizing his vision, glass is a natural. However, rather than using unbroken expanses of glazing, it is most typical of his residential design to use groupings of smaller windows, as in these three Connecticut homes.

"To me, glass is the keynote to our ability in modern times to relate to the surroundings and take advantage of the sun's movement," he says. "On the other hand, not a lot of people can feel totally at ease when completely surrounded by glass, devoid of a sense of protective shelter. That is why, although I use a great deal of glass, I tend to use groupings of windows rather than monstrous sheets of glass, which also are less economical as they require special handling. Also, by grouping the

For this northeastern Connecticut home commanding fine views, Alfredo De Vido faced the exterior walls with stock clad windows under a wide, sheltering, saltbox-shaped roof that reflects the area's Colonial context. The pattern of the many small-scale windows also conveys a traditional feeling, as does the dramatic entry provided by the French doors.

Photography by Paul Warchol

This house was built to take advantage of vistas to the distant woods and lake below through a wide terrace for outside viewing and ample windows for the hours spent inside. Windows are placed in a pattern within the shapes of the house, heightening the impact of each. To provide yet another perspective, the stairs rise toward a curving wall of glass block.

Photography by Frederick Charles

windows you hold the wall visually through the grid of mullions and patterns, making it part of the enclosing wall. On the domestic scale, where one large sheet of glass can get a little institutional, groups of smaller windows can be arranged to make a pattern in the exterior wall, thereby containing the interior space and at the same time letting the occupants of the rooms see out. The idea is to bring the outside inside but at the same time give a sense of shelter."

The site was a steep hill for this home with a fine view to a lake below. To maximize the view from the house, glass, set within a basic wood frame clad in white cedar siding, was stepped back from the bottom to the top. This stepping arrangement also enabled the expansive house to assume a more domestic scale, and the stepped-back roofs serve to brace the glass against the strong winds that blow in gusts across the lake.

Photography by Paul Warchol

FORTRESS IN GLASS

Laminated Glass & Glass Block

On one side this home in Colavita, Italy, is built like a brick fortress to reflect the imposing strength of its nearest neighboring structure, a medieval castle. Yet on the other side, which descends five stories down a hillside with expansive views of the distant town, architect **Angelo Tartaglia** did a complete about-face by turning almost every wall into glass.

LAMINATED GLASS: *"Visarm" by Saint Gobain*
GLASS BLOCK: *Fidenza Vetraria s.p.a.*

ABOVE LEFT   *In the kitchen, the heaviness of the fortress theme continuing in the shape of the windows is lightened by the marble's whiteness.*

ABOVE   *In a bathroom, light as well as privacy is preserved through the extensive use of opaque and clear glass block.*

LEFT & OPPOSITE   *In all rooms of the house, windows looking out toward a neighboring medieval castle were inspired by its strong simple shape as well as its fortress-like nature. Yet on the side of the house overlooking the valley, the architect capitalized on the expansive view by designing enormous windows and making the walls on this side floor-to-ceiling sliding doors of laminated glass. To create the feeling of even more lightness, glass is also used for furniture, shelving and stair rails.*

Photography by Edoardo D'Antona

LIGHT PASSAGES

Stained Glass

The residence of Siraj Alhamrani in Jeddah, Saudi Arabia, is filled with the special glow created only through the soft, multidimensional and multicolored quality of stained glass. A primary element in this house by Milanese architect **Franco Audrito**, its watercolor hues were edited from five hundred samples sent to interior designer **Christopher Rebman** of Washington, D.C.

Rebman selected twenty-five of the coolest colors of those samples to serve as an aesthetic and psychological relief from the surrounding desert palette and heat. In fact, the stained glass was actually used as one might use watercolors, with glass of various hues superimposed on others to create new shades. The resulting soft tones he reflected in all interior furnishings and finishes, continuing the architect's vision of a refreshing and lyrical visual poem throughout.

GLASS ARTISAN AND MANUFACTURER: *Arte & Vetro*

LEFT *Inside, similar stained glass separates entry hall from formal and family living areas, thus adding a second level of privacy.*

ABOVE *Between the front garden and the formal and family halls, extensive walls of handmade stained glass filter the view.*

Photography by Matteo Piazza

Stained-glass walls introduce a sense of mystery and a desire for discovery, in this way replacing in this contemporary architecture the traditional Moslem wooden screens.

SUNLIGHT AND MOONBEAMS

Tempered Glass, Glass Block & Mirror

Overlooking the picturesque Chattahoochee River in Georgia, this home by architect **Robert Whitfield** and interior designer **Louis Shuster** makes the most of its views of the lush forests and winding river beyond, as well as the clients' preference for natural light and reflective materials. With their plentiful use of glass, the designers heightened the sense of sun, water, sky and earth throughout the Mediterranean/Southwest structure and, aided by a lighting system which makes the reflective surfaces sparkle well past sundown, enlivened it with a spirited transparency day and night.

RIGHT *A domed, indirectly lighted skylight illuminates the entry round-the-clock, while the glass door and clerestory windows begin the progression of glorious views from a multitude of angles.*

Photography by Kim Sargent

WINDOWS: *Pella of Georgia*
SKYLIGHTS: *Sunglow Skylight Products*
SPECIALTY GLASS WORK: *Atlanta Glasscrafters*
WINDOWS AT TOP OF FOYER AND ALL MIRROR WORK: **North Fulton Glass**
FROSTED AND ETCHED GLASS ON LAP POOL DOORS: *Farallon Studios, Inc.*

Three-story walls of glass in the "great room" allow panoramic views to feel like extensions of the space, while glass-topped tables continue the material inside for a sense of continuity and further spaciousness.

LEFT & ABOVE *Domed, indirectly lighted skylights in the lap pool area allow sun, moon and stars to take the place of ceilings. Sunburst patterns imbedded in glass block increase their refracted brilliance. The glass door is frosted and etched.*

RIGHT *Tempered glass, mirror and glass block provide a play of light in the master bathroom, its foil a wealth of Rojo Alicante marble and natural maple.*

LIGHT MUSIC

Low-E Argon-Filled Glass

The area's wooded landscape on an island in Maine is essential to environmentalist Nan Miller. So are natural light and being able to trace its movement from sunup to sundown, spring to winter. So is freedom from the myriad natural and man-made substances to which she is acutely allergic.

Designed by architect **Peter Forbes** with associates **Gerard A. Gutierrez, Barry Dallas, Bradford C. Walker** and interior designer **Christine Maclin**, the home's absence of barriers between indoors, outdoors and even between floors creates a seamless harmony. As Forbes describes it, "Spaces flow together and one is so immediately surrounded by the forest while inside the house that, upon going outside, it is often a shock to find a coat is necessary."

Environmental responsibility plays a major part in his architectural composition as well. Endangered species have been carefully avoided. The glass is oriented to light and heats the space as much as possible naturally, and the roof is angled to deflect wind

LOW-E ARGON-FILLED GLASS (USED THROUGHOUT): *Libby Owens Ford*
GLASS PANELS: *Sisco*
WINDOW WALL ASSEMBLAGE: *American Glass*
WINDOWS: *Modu-Line Windows*
ALUMINUM SLIDING DOORS: *Arcadia Manufacturing Inc.*

Ascent to the sleeping quarters is offered by a twenty-three-foot-long staircase and a red-framed glass elevator.

and cold. There are no materials which are toxic or allergenic. And air is constantly being exchanged throughout the house, a factor enhanced by the open spaces allowing fresh air to circulate freely.

The free space itself is ordered by the home's structure. An armature of steel tubes defines and organizes the soaring volume, gently directs circulation, subtly defines functions and provides a framework for the constantly changing mementos of Nan Miller's life, friends and family. The walls of glass and aluminum similarly orchestrate, but never inhibit, the fullest experience of the tree-surrounded, sun-filled environment.

A crystal pavilion intimately at one with its island setting, the house embraces the forest's play of light in a visual symphony of reflections, refractions and shadows.

ABOVE LEFT *The steel frame casts its pattern and, in turn, receives the lattice of shadows cast by the window wall.*

ABOVE RIGHT *The elevator, designed by architect Peter Forbes, arrives at the second level's guest bedroom and bath.*

OPPOSITE *The steel staircase, ascending past a wall of windows and the naturescape beyond, becomes a spiral between second and third levels.*

*Awning windows open to allow
Maine's fresh breezes to circulate
through bath and sleeping areas.*

UNVEILING THE VIEW

Tempered Glass & Fiberglass

When Venice Atelier Architects' **James P. Wright** was asked to rebuild a residence destroyed in the 1992 Oakland fire storm, he used glass and fiberglass in response to the site's special features — an entry six feet below the level of the street as well as a magnificent view of the cityscape beyond.

To counteract the expectation of a cave-like enclosure when descending to a home's front door, he used translucent wall and ceiling panels in the entry vestibule, creating a space filled with light while maintaining privacy from the street. Adding to the warm welcome is the garden that commences at the street and that, with the architecture, provides a sense of meticulously defined procession that continues inside as they alternately veil and unveil each interior and exterior view along the home's central core. At the same time, that transparent core serves the home's six different levels as a luminous hub day and night.

TEMPERED GLASS: *Blomberg Window Systems*
TRANSLUCENT PANEL SYSTEM: *Kalwall, distributed by Collier Building Specialties*

ABOVE & OPPOSITE *At night the atrium has illumination cast on the exterior, thus turning street-facing walls into a privacy screen.*

LEFT *The central core of glass and fiberglass weaves its sense of transparency into six rooms on six different levels.*

RIGHT *From the rear garden at night, the generous number and variety of windows turn the house into a multifaceted lantern.*

Photography by Anthony Peres

ARTSCAPE

Tempered Glass

It is as if the house had been designed expressly for Jane Gottlieb's painted photography and digital fine art. Every wall and ceiling is pierced with glass, letting the sun make the most of her works' rainbow hues and the structure's corresponding palette. The fact of the matter is, however, that architect **W. Douglas Breidenbach** built this single family dwelling on a tight infill lot in Southern California as a speculative venture. Yet rather than play it safe, he followed his idea of what would be right architecturally in terms of the site, fully aware he was limiting his market.

As in all of Breidenbach's work, a major design consideration was the creation of light-filled spaces that flow together in a dynamic and dramatic fashion. To do that here, on property located deep in Santa Monica Canyon seemingly miles away from the urban milieu and including mature specimen trees, meant creating a flow that would integrate exterior and interior completely.

"The location of the existing trees made the solution somewhat predestined," says Breidenbach. The public spaces were placed at the rear, forming the perimeter of

ABOVE & OPPOSITE *The sizes, heights and positions of the doors and windows achieve a tremendous amount of interplay between exterior and interior, with the variety of the views creating a playful, magical mood that seems created especially for the joyous feeling of Jane Gottlieb's art.*

LEFT *Since the property is located deep within a canyon, the idea of the landscape was to recreate a canyon stream.*

Photography by Jane Gottlieb

SKYLIGHT: *Acralight*
DOORS AND WINDOWS: *through T.M. Cobb/Ventana Distributing*
VINYL WINDOWS: *Mirage Vinyl Doors & Windows*

The structure's ample glazing has been planned to sensitively frame the garden views.

The living, dining and family rooms form the perimeter of the garden and, due to the extensive glazing, benefit from its lush beauty as well as privacy. The sofa is from Saporiti Italia. The rug, designed by Gottlieb, was produced by Jazz.

LEFT *The entry, a two-story space
illuminated by a continuous ridge
skylight, serves as the home's primary gallery for Jane Gottlieb's
painted photography and digital
fine art.*

BELOW *The continuous ridge
skylight over the two story gallery
space turns its top level into a
room suited for sunning as well
as viewing.*

the garden, which is a re-creation of a
canyon stream. The stream flows through
the space, passing underneath a bridge con-
necting the entry with the living room.

The introduction of the various wood-
framed glass doors, windows and fixed glazing serves to relate the outside to the inside
while carefully framing the views for maximum aesthetic effect. In addition, since the
deep canyon setting can mitigate the
amount of natural sunlight reaching the
house, a continuous ridge skylight was cen-
tered over the two-story entry.

"I knew only highly individualistic
people would wind up buying this house,
but for them it would be ideal," he says.
And for Gottlieb, who added the structure's
colorful palette after purchase, and her
husband David Obst, it is.

ALL-EMBRACING SERENITY

Tempered Solar-Bronze Glass

This thoroughly contemporary home exudes a sense of remarkable quiet, privacy and serenity — all carefully predetermined by the architectural firm of **Buff, Smith & Hensman** and interior designer **Sheri Schlesinger.**

A heavily traveled street serving the property as well as neighbors on the remaining three sides dictated acoustic as well as visual privacy. This was established through the use of a series of walled and landscaped areas functioning as baffles and clearly developing the site in its entirety for maximum use, with all major interior volumes expanding into commensurate garden spaces.

To create the flow from interior to exterior, glass was the major element, with all major rooms visually expanded horizontally and vertically by views to the garden and sky. Glass also allowed for the play of light, shade and shadow to add interest and excitement to the architecture, and, since the glass is frameless, the illusion of no separation between indoors and out is maximized. Mitered glass corners exaggerate the illusion of openness as well.

"Glass is a paradox," notes **Donald C. Hensman**. "It's something you add to a structure but cannot see, yet, for a relatively low cost, it accomplishes so much."

RIGHT *At night, glass continues its role in the architectural juxtaposition of positive and negative spaces.*

BELOW *A mitered glass corner exaggerates the open feeling in a way not possible when corner mullions exist.*

Photography by Mary E. Nichols

*The illusion of no separation
between interior and exterior gives
pool and garden areas the feeling
of being huge and airy pavilions
comfortably connected to the house.*

FIRE AND ICE

Pressed Glass

I t would seem an impossibility to find in one material two opposite attributes and then celebrate them in one functional form. Yet within his own home in Mexico City, architect **Agustin Hernandez** has managed to express both the fire-like brilliance and the icy depths of glass.

GLASS AND TABLE BASE: *fabricated in the studio of Agustin Hernandez*

ABOVE *The same pressed-glass technique used for the dining table is used for the piece over the fireplace, except instead of the glass being glued to stainless steel, the base is made of concrete. The location, over the fireplace and opposite a garden that lets in much natural light during the day, is ideal for making the most of the reflective character of the glass, which also is used to counterpoint the architecture's curved lines and the fabrics' soft feel.*

LEFT & OPPOSITE *A dining table, made of four- by half-inch pieces of glass which have been pressed together and joined by clear adhesive, extends six meters in length and is cantilevered to a single support of stainless steel. For such a large piece of heavy material, the result is surprisingly light in appearance.*

Photography by Tim Street-Porter

DECORATIVE MAGIC

Mirror & Etched Glass

A room by *James Blakeley III* is always a lesson in decorative magic, full of the imaginative uses of materials he has spent his career discovering. Here, he has turned to glass and its myriad possible forms to create the highly graceful, richly decorative and ever-inventive interiors for which he is known.

"In the garden room, we were presented with an elegant space, two walls of which were enhanced by French doors and molding. The problem was that the other two walls were composed of very typical sliding glass doors. By exchanging them with etched glass panels, we were able to carry out the beauty and proportion established by the doors and molding at the opposing walls. The magic of glass is that we could do all this without interfering with the view."

MIRROR AND ETCHED GLASS: *UltraGlas, Inc.*

BELOW: *Floor-to-ceiling mirror without baseboards or ceiling crowns makes walls seem to disappear in this small master bath which now looks as if it has infinite space. Here, objects themselves become the focal point, with holes cut into the mirror to receive the picture and the acrylic shelves.*

Photography by Christopher Covey

The former sliding glass doors with aluminum frames never did complement this otherwise elegant garden room, so James Blakeley exchanged them for expansive panels of etched glass. The design of the etching corresponds to the French doors and molding and balances their height.

URBAN
REFRACTIONS

Jim Olson

Joseph Braswell

Jean-Pierre Heim

Aldo Vandini

Powell/Kleinschmidt

Reginald Adams

Carl D'Aquino & Paul Laird

Thomas Hanrahan & Victoria Meyers

Brian E. Kaye & J. Kevin Gray

Christian Grimonprez

Margaret Helfand & Marti Cowan

Warren Carther

David Hertz

EXPERIMENT IN LIGHT AND SPACE

Tempered, Slumped, Fused & Cast Glass

The condominium of architect **Jim Olson** and his wife Katherine is an experiment in art, light and space, a sanctuary from the surrounding urban buzz of Seattle's historic Pioneer Square. Designed by Olson during a thoughtful process in which he invited sculptor **Nancy Mee** and artist **Jeffrey Bishop** to attend planning meetings, the interior is completely integrated with a number of commissioned works of art that become a part of the living experience itself.

LEFT *Jeffrey Bishop's twenty-foot oil-on-canvas mural provides a brilliantly-colored backdrop for Nancy Mee's sculptures of slumped and fused glass with welded steel armatures and copper.*

BELOW *Art reflected in the living room's expansive glass window walls melts into the nighttime views of Seattle, giving the space a sense of infinity.*

Photography by Michael Ian Shopenn

In the middle of the Olson residence, in which every space has
been carefully planned to provide
an axial relationship with art, the
stairs ascend to a mid-level niche
enlivened by R. Niemi's "Metal
Man" and various sculptures,
mostly religious figures, from a
diversity of cultures.

Photography by Dick Busher

Whereas city lights tend to predominate at night, the art seems to envelope the space during daylight hours.

Photography by
Michael Ian Shopenn

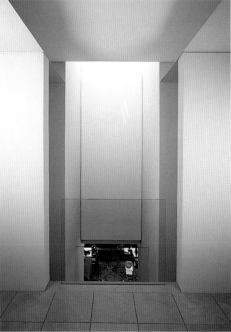

ABOVE & OPPOSITE *The kitchen back-splash is turned into art by Ann Gardner's cast glass tiles with copper inclusions.*

FAR LEFT & LEFT *Sheets of tempered glass embedded in the floor become stair railings.*

Photography above and left by Michael Ian Shopenn

Photography far left and opposite by Dick Busher

CUSTOM STAIR RAILINGS: *Burt Lockhart/Jerry Fulks and Company*

A TRANSLUCENT ATELIER

Mirror, Glass & Lucite

The concept behind the plan of this duplex apartment in New York City was extremely popular during the 1920s when it was built. The front double-story living room with single-story chambers on two levels in the rear produced the feeling of an atelier that is still completely charming. Nonetheless, this one had been sorely neglected and it was **Joseph Braswell's** task to totally reconstruct the space while preserving its original mood.

With his deft incorporation of new technology as well as a monochromatic color scheme, his typical preference, the fifteen-foot-wide residence looks as spacious as an ocean liner. In fact, it comes as no surprise to learn that Braswell has designed many ships and also planes. He attributes his experience designing various projects that float and fly, where space is at an even greater premium, to making him so sure-footed on land!

MIRROR INSTALLATION: *Sundial-Schwartz, Inc.*
SPUTNIK LIGHTING FIXTURE: *designed by Joseph Braswell, fabricated by Louis Baldinger & Sons*
COFFEE AND OCCASIONAL TABLES: *Karl Springer Ltd.*

ABOVE *In a conversation area, mirror surrounds an eighteenth-century English cabinet, thus extending the sense of space in a small area. As the mirror is only on this one wall and not the opposing one, the challenge of "double infinity" does not arise. A controlled color palette and other reflective surfaces, including stainless steel, also contribute to the sense of spacious serenity.*

LEFT *In the master bedroom, which is no larger than a stateroom on an ocean liner, mirror seems to expand the space.*

Photography by Jaime Ardiles-Arce

The fascia of the balcony railing is sheathed in mirror to relieve a sense of enclosure. The Thai silk used for the portiere curtains framing the balcony as well as the double-story panels in the living room provides an important sense of softness.

The large window in the living room is dressed with a casement blind made of wool challis that is operated mechanically and illuminated at night to avoid the feeling of a large black hole. An updated and overscaled version of Sputnik, a lighting fixture Joseph Braswell originally designed in the 1950s, was fabricated of Lucite radiant fiber-optic rods which create a sense of expansion in the lofty room. A pair of framed paper sculptures by Nancy Miller are placed vis-à-vis on two facing mirrored walls, thus eliminating the disturbing sense of "double infinity" (too much reflection) while still creating a sense of extended space.

COMMON MATERIALS, UNCOMMON MIX

Frosted Glass, Tempered Glass & Mirror

Aldo Vandini, founder of the interdisciplinary firm Koaladesign, is noted for his highly original approach, and nothing could exemplify it more than this penthouse located in the historic center of Bologna.

Throwing to the winds all reverence for the past, he used common industrial components throughout. His redesign fully utilizes the restricted space, narrow and deep as is  typical of the area's town houses. Rows of brick pillars along longitudinal perimeters were replaced by columns made of laminated wood. In turn, this led to further space-saving devices, such as furnishing the empty spaces between the pillars with cabinetry. Splined tubular aluminum profiles, usually used in conveyor belt platforms of automatic units, were employed to support bookshelves and kitchen storage. In the bathroom located on the mezzanine, he detailed teak floors and walls with a pattern created by thick aluminum plates. And throughout, the idea of borrowing light from adjacent spaces in order to illuminate closed interior rooms led to his use of typical tempered glass in various atypical ways.

In the entry, Vandini inserted into the wall two windows of double-paned glass, between which venetian blinds are sandwiched to provide privacy, to capture the natural light from the stairwell. For the wall between the bathroom and living room, he used slightly frosted glass so as to exploit all

A mirrored wardrobe enables the bedroom to serve as dressing area.

Photography by Janos Grapow

FAR LEFT & ABOVE *Glass is used as structure to divide living and bathroom areas.*

LEFT *Wide horizontal bands of frosted glass punctuated by one clear band form the bathroom door, while a window facing into the stairwell is provided with venetian blinds for privacy.*

The bathroom sited on the lower floor of the penthouse, devised as a sort of crossing point to be reached from both the living room and the bedroom, incorporates a frosted glass wall to borrow natural light from the adjacent area. Frosted and clear glass panels divide the room into two communicating areas, one housing the washbowl, the toilet and laundry equipment, and one hosting shower, bath and bidet.

The addition of a sliding glass window fills the kitchen/dining area with sunlight for the greater part of the day.

existing natural light into windowless areas. And he converted an entire brick wall along the kitchen/dining area into one of sliding glass, turning the sunlit space into an extension of the terrace beyond.

"Of course, there is always compromise," he says. "Everything you see resulted from adjusting my personal needs to the rooms at my disposal. However, far from limiting my creativity, such problems allowed me to study and experiment with alternative solutions. For much the same reason I admire the design of sailing boats, I enjoy the need to organize space rationally and to treat every square inch as essential. Such prerequisites teach us to live in unity with the surrounding world by ruling out any waste and allowing for few useless items."

In the end, though no remnants from the past remain inside, the addition of the steel-framed windows makes the view of Bologna's layered history more accessible than ever and, due to the juxtaposition of old with new, seemingly more precious as well.

FROSTED AND TEMPERED GLASS: *Saint Gobain through Vetreria Corticella Felsinia srl.*

SIMPLICITY IN CHICAGO

Tempered & Frosted Glass

Inspired by this Chicago apartment's location within a 1919 skyscraper designed by Ludwig Mies van der Rohe, **Robert D. Kleinschmidt** and **Donald D. Powell** used as much glass within as the architect used without. Paying further homage to their mentor, they reflected the curves of a skyscraper designed by Mies van der Rohe in 1919 (and which can be seen from the windows) in the biomorphic shape they gave a glass-topped banquette unit dividing the dining area. The uninterrupted flow of this and other luminous glass designs in the rooms beyond exemplify these designers' ability to achieve admirable simplicity of line and form.

With its frosted glass top concealing fluorescent tubes, this unit that separates dining and corridor areas also serves as a light box. For the unit's form, made of particleboard coated with polyurethane lacquer, the designers chose blue to refer to the apartment's site on Lake Michigan. On most days, the windows are left unadorned to capitalize on maximum light penetration and the view. However, when glare does occur, Mecho-Shades, concealed in the gray mesh, can be lowered, and when evenings are cold, the gray silk drapery can be drawn across the entire window wall for a sense of protective warmth.

GLASS-TOPPED BANQUETTE UNIT: *Designed by Powell/Kleinschmidt, fabricated by Parenti & Raffaelli*

Photography by Jon Miller, Hedrich-Blessing

GRACE NOTES

Carved, Etched & Tempered Glass

A formal elegance transcends every home designed by **Reginald Adams**. Whether the architecture is palatial in scale and motif or simply a post-and-beam contemporary structure whose clients hunger for more decorative magic, he is noted for elevating each property through his orchestration of rich and highly worked materials. The result always is a visually elaborate symphony, and one that depends on decorative glass for many of its most sparkling highlights.

FIREPLACE SCREEN & DINING ENTRY: *Trilogy Glass Design*

RIGHT *The glowing flames backlight this fireplace screen, highlighting its carved and etched surface. The glass used throughout the residence has been tempered for safety reasons.*

Photography by Mary E. Nichols

A mirrored ceiling seems to double the height of this enchanting dining room, while the carved and etched glass surrounding the entry visually extends its length. Placing each shih *(Chinese sculptured lion) on acrylic rather than granite pedestals further enhances the sense of airy spaciousness.*

In another urban residence, Carl D'Aquino and Paul Laird, Architect, have created an atmosphere of nineteenth-century elegance. Throughout the custom-designed kitchen, bleached ash cabinets with antique leaded glass doors provide a subtle period feeling. And entry to the barrel-vaulted hall with its bold painting by Pablo Picasso is through equally dramatic doors, designed by D'Aquino and Laird with **Dennis Abbe** to include an Empire pattern etched in glass.

Photography by George Mott

FOYER DOORS: **Dennis Abbe**
ANTIQUE GLASS FOR CUSTOM CABINETRY: *supplied by S.A. Bendheim, Inc., fabricated by Rambusch*

In the renovation of a three-bedroom residence on Park Avenue, the pre-war floorplan was gutted to create a bright, cleanly detailed classical look. Project designer with Carl D'Aquino Interiors and Paul Laird, Architect was **Jaime Vasquez**.

The glass-block bedroom was designed around the requirements of a young man bound for college. Converted from what had previously been two maids' rooms, fixed riser columns presented a challenge that was turned to an advantage by fitting them with stereo speakers and a television. In addition, the columns delineate the boundaries of the bed and join to a platform and a dresser. The curved glass block wall serves both as a light source and bathroom enclosure, within which glass tile carries forth the room's luminosity.

Photography by George Mott

ABOVE *For an apartment in Harperley Hall, a residence built at the turn of the century in the Craftsman style, Carl D'Aquino Interiors and **Geordi Humphreys** maintained the period feeling through the kind of materials used and the way they used them.*

The bath for the mistress of the house is distinguished by leaded-glass doors, a gracefully curving custom sink counter with chrome-legged base, huge slabs of black marble typical of the period's hotels, and ample mirror to double the effect.

Photography by John Hall

FREE FLOW

Tempered & Sandblasted Glass

There is only one full-height wall in this total renovation of an industrial loft space in lower Manhattan, and that one wall is made of glass. The design intention was to achieve the ultimate degree of transparency and spatial fluidity possible, and architects **Thomas Hanrahan** and **Victoria Meyers** did it.

Their client knew he wanted to escape from his tightly-scheduled professional days into a peacefully uncluttered, pared-down space. He also was partial to Hanrahan & Meyers' previous projects that explored ambiguities between exterior and interior by means of partial enclosures and transparent materials. The more they discussed what to do with this space, its 3,800 square feet previously subdivided into fourteen rooms for a family with young children, the more the design began to assume a dispersed and radically open character. In the end, they were left with no solid walls whatsoever, save for that one single, full-height glass-and-steel divider marking off the master bedroom and bath from the rest of the apartment. Even there, unless the curtains are drawn, the intention is to reveal the full dimension of the entire space. Even the furnishings found or commissioned by interior designer Tse-Yun Chu are minimal in number and minimalist in design so as not to interrupt the flow.

RIGHT & BELOW *To answer the need for acoustic separation, a full-height wall of glass and raw steel divides the master bedroom and bath from the rest of the loft space. For visual privacy, a curtain can be drawn over the glass wall.*

Photography © Peter Aarons/Esto

SANDBLASTED GLASS: *Exquisite Glass & Stone, Inc.*
CURVED GLASS: *Flickinger Glassworks, Inc.*

LEFT *Walls of glass and raw steel separate the loft's main area overlooking Broadway from the kitchen on the left and, on the right, from the master bedroom and bath.*

To further facilitate the openness, cabinetry is kept low and panels are movable. "The idea was to not construct walls but to make rooms via the cabinetry," says Hanrahan. This final aspect of the architects' innovative plan yields, for all its uncluttered simplicity, a complex space of constantly changing perspectives and points of view. The movable panels allow for the creation of smaller, more intimate spaces to accommodate overnight guests, while their partial height permits light from both sides of the apartment to penetrate deep into all areas of the residence, creating further visual transmutations, sunup to sundown.

ABOVE AND RIGHT *For overnight guests, movable partitions enable three bedrooms to be made of one. Made of painted wood, these panels also provide privacy.*

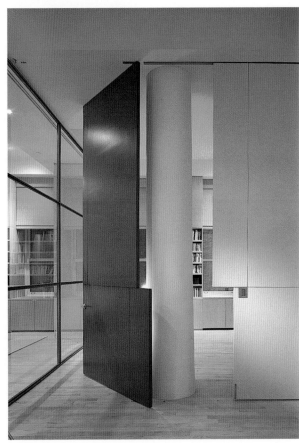

ABOVE *The view from the Broadway side of the apartment reveals the exceeding transparency of the main living space.*

LEFT & RIGHT *Nothing but a thirty-foot-long maple cabinet defines the kitchen, while other areas are framed by slender steel beams.*

PENTHOUSE WITH A '50S TWIST

Glass Tile, Mirror, Frosted & Tempered Glass

Glass was a natural consideration in transfusing a dark penthouse apartment in New York City with a contemporary, open feeling for fashion designer Wolfgang Joop and his collection of mid-twentieth-century French furnishings. Yet it is the way in which the glass has been used by architect **Brian E. Kaye** and decorator **J. Kevin Gray**, two designers always seeking to use elements and finishes in nontraditional ways, that makes the definitive difference. The new perspectives they bring to design are ideally suited to Joop's own taste. All three like colors that are warm, shapes that are bold and materials that are irresistible ... yet in such highly edited combinations that, in the end, what is warm, bold and irresistible seems serene as well.

RIGHT *Mirrored closet doors in the dressing room provide the simplest, most direct answer to lightening a dark space — as well as a splendid way to double the effect of the Lianne lamp by Royère.*

Photography by Deidi von Schaewen

GOLD-LEAFED MOSAIC TILE: *manufactured by Bizazza s.p.a./supplied by Nemo Tile, installed by Gramar Industries*
SKYLIGHT AND WINDOW WALL IN STUDY: *Shading Systems Inc.*

BELOW *In the study, glass doors leading to the terrace as well as a new skylight/window wall open the apartment to views of the city and make this study one of the sunniest spots in Manhattan. The total renovation of this room included the designers' custom-designed shelving/storage units and specification of new flooring, finishes, furniture and lighting.*

RIGHT *Turquoise walls are enlivened with a fireplace surround of 24-karat gold Venetian glass tile and custom-designed bronze-framed mirrors. The result maintains a sense of elevated classicism that relates to the collection of mid-twentieth-century French furnishings. Flanking the fireplace are Jean Royère chairs, in front of it is a coffee table by Jean Prouvé and a Royère chaise, and over the eclectic addition of an eighteenth-century Venetian console table is a 1940 painting by Lempicka,* Girl with Teddy Bear.

ON THE EDGE IN BELGIUM

Tempered & Acid-Etched Glass

When architect **Christian Grimonprez** and photographer Nike Bourgeois decided to build right in the center of Roeselare, Belgium, adjacent to the town's oldest and most traditional structures, they resolved what appeared to be numerous spatial restrictions with distinction.

Their main idea was to give the structure a completely different appearance from the other buildings in town — a progressive identity suitable for his architectural studio on the ground floor and for her studio and home on the top three floors.

The result in Bourgeois' section is shown here — with forms, lines, materials, spatial organization and technical details that are not merely progressive but highly experimental. Walls and even floors move, creating an enormous degree of changeability. Work spaces become dining/living areas, which in turn become the master bedroom. The reality of flexibility is extended further by maintaining few furnishings. Those that do exist are of a transient nature — all are movable, changeable and storable.

Capping the feeling of "let's not be burdened by too much permanence and too many possessions" are the simplest of materials — terracotta-colored plaster, blue industrial polyurethane floors, and aluminum and glass everywhere.

TEMPERED GLASS: *Saint-Roch*
ACID-ETCHED GLASS: *D.B.I.*

LEFT *As the project is completely built between other buildings, the facade, together with the roof surface, are the only points from which daylight could be brought inside — a factor prompting Christian Grimonprez to construct the building predominantly of double glazing in aluminum frames.*

BELOW & OPPOSITE *Encased with glass on three sides, Nike Bourgeois' multifunctional space on the fourth level is a greenhouse for living.*

Photography by Nike Bourgeois

The second floor has a ceiling 5.5 meters (18 feet) high with a movable aluminum mezzanine. Since the mezzanine floor can move, it is possible to have the morning sun stream in from the street side on the east or move it away from the windows at night. Sliding partitions of acid-etched glass framed with aluminum serve as walls, providing a look of Japanese shoji screens and allowing the sun to reach deep into the home-and-studio's furthest areas. In addition, the prevalent transparent aesthetic complements the effortlessly changeable feeling derived from the movability of walls and floor, a feeling further enhanced by simple, movable and storable furnishings.

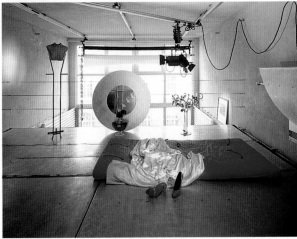

A MOVABLE SYSTEM

*Seeded Hand-Blown, Clear, Acid-Etched & Industrial
Ribbed Pressed Glass*

Limited space can lead to ingenious solutions. This was the case when **Margaret Helfand** and **Marti Cowan** of Margaret Helfand Architects remodeled a one-bedroom trapezoidal pied-a-terre overlooking New York City's East River.

Although occupying only a thousand square feet, the apartment was to provide storage and display for owner Diane Bliss's extensive collection of books and art as well as serve other needs — including offering a dining area that could double as a home office and a living room that could convert occasionally into a guest room.

Limitation of space for storage meant that much of the wall area would be devoted to cabinetwork, while the need for separation and privacy as well as a sunscreen led to the invention of a movable translucent wall panel system, that is itself a work of art.

ABOVE & OPPOSITE *Separation and privacy are created by a system of intersecting steel and glass rolling panels. The panels comprise a collage of three layers of glass, with each layer being a different trapezoidal shape to reflect the geometry of the floor plan and cabinetwork. Each layer is also of a different texture, thereby contrasting translucent hand-blown seeded glass, industrial-ribbed pressed glass and clear glass.*

RIGHT *Walls of the dining and living areas received cherrywood bookcases, partially covered with doors in some areas to create a rhythm of solid and void woodwork. A full-height, deep, two-way cabinet was located between living and dining areas to create a passageway as well as accommodate a concealed desk on one side and space for a television cart, sound system and bar on the other.*

Photography by Paul Warchol

ABOVE *Starting at the entry, light is the topic of exploration in this project where space was extremely limited but views and light are abundant. Being the ideal vehicle to access both view and light, glass was used to provide a flexible system of dividing and defining space, to invite light into the interior of the apartment, and to provide continuity with the solid and void rhythm of the cabinetwork.*

GENERAL CONTRACTOR AND FABRICATOR OF CUSTOM GLASS DOORS, CABINETWORK, TABLES, STEEL AND DOOR LEVERS: **Mark Hill Fabrications Inc.**
LIGHT FIXTURES: **Harold Lehr**

NOVEL ACCENTS

Tempered Glass, Glass Block & Laminated Glass

The uses of glass are as unbounded as one's imagination, and architect **David Hertz** seems inspired to try them all. Whether creating collages of cocktail stirrers and eyeglass lenses, eliminating frames from shower doors or mixing glass with Syndecrete®, the precast lightweight concrete product he has developed, Hertz is ever enlivening his tautly functional design with head-turning innovation.

RIGHT *In the Keith Lehrer residence in Bel Air, California, a sheet of half-inch tempered glass serves as a dividing screen between toilet and vanity. The frameless glass, which is integrated into the floor, walls and ceiling, is of one piece, with the Syndecrete and wood counter, cut in two pieces, appearing to pass through it.*

Photography by Tom Bonner

GLASS BLOCK: *Pittsburgh Corning Corporation*
TEMPERED GLASS: *Tempwerks*
LAMINATED GLASS: *Asahi Glass Company Limited through AMA Glass Corporation*

LEFT *An operable steel window in a glass block wall allows for ventilation and a view of the landscape beyond.*

Photography by Marvin Rand

ABOVE *For an uncluttered look, this glass shower enclosure has been inserted into reveals which have been cast in the tub made of Syndecrete lightweight concrete. With the reveals providing support and the custom designed pivot hinges inserted into the glass itself, the glass door needs no frame. To allow diffused light to enter the space, the architect cast acrylic rods into a wall of Syndecrete.*

Photography by Tom Bonner

Rice paper-laminated Asahi glass gives privacy while providing a foil for natural light and shadows. Clear glass is used at the top to extend the view.

Photography by Tom Bonner

A RESPECTFUL ADDITION

Tempered Glass

Raphael S. Soriano was a highly respected modernist California architect, his steel frame homes recognized for their straightforward simplicity derived from his rare ability to find the most precisely suitable architectural form for industry's latest products. Therefore **Ronald W. Aarons** used great restraint when remodeling a 1950 Soriano home in Los Angeles. Although he completely gutted, remodeled and amplified its original one-story structure and added a new two-story wing to meet the clients' need for an extensive library and office, he never ignored the original design.

Aarons maintained his predecessor's ten-foot building module and continued the use of the same type of steel framing structure Soriano had used, thereby allowing for the elimination of all window jambs and headers so that walls facing the garden could be completely made of glass. These two aspects were essential to Aarons in his remodeling and new addition, allowing this home to live on as an exemplary work of modern architecture.

As part of the remodel, the ceiling was raised and clerestory windows were added, allowing natural light to penetrate into the foyer.

Photography by Anthony Peres

GENERAL CONTRACTOR: *Coughlin Builders*
LIBRARY SKYLIGHT: *Pacific Skylights*
GLASS DOORS, WINDOWS AND OTHER SKYLIGHTS: *Terry Sash and Door*
LARGE SLIDING GLASS AND FIXED GLASS WINDOWS: *Fleetwood Aluminum*

The new addition includes a research library housing fifteen thousand volumes and provides work space for a full-time librarian and research assistant. A major skylight was incorporated to expose the contents of the library to natural light for easy reading and quick reference of book titles.

The contemporary office environment adjacent to the library was designed to take advantage of the abundant natural light and views of the lush garden beyond.

LEFT *The two-story library addition is at the heart of the house, easily accessed from the two working offices by spiral stair or elevator.*

ABOVE *The original building was gutted, and what was once the entire house is now one spacious entry/living/dining area. As in the original structure, the steel framing was concealed in the ceiling and the doorjambs were designed flush with the walls, resulting in completely floor-to-ceiling and wall-to-wall openings of glass. Soon after the renovation was completed, the strength of the steel structural frame supporting the dual glazed sliding glass doors was tested by the Northridge earthquake of January 17, 1994. No damage was sustained.*

The use of glass walls and skylights illuminates the new two-story library addition and opens all rooms of the house to a view of the lushly landscaped yards and pool. Out of respect for the original architect's design intent, Ron Aarons adhered to the ten-foot structural module established by the spaces between the original column grid.

H

Te

V

in

ex

pla

an

cla

fas

wa

im

sep

on

Vis

to

ca

In

red

tu

the

ma

say

bo

in

no

Pho

ABOVE *Furnishings create an interplay of rectilinear planes unattached to the transparent exterior wall.*

RIGHT *Throughout the residence, the elimination of closures at some ceiling planes makes walls seem to float and, in the master bath, a freestanding shower wall shows no evidence of support whatsoever.*

STE

by

GEN

Honed white Thassos marble slabs used as bases for the collection of African sculpture allow their shapes to stand in stark relief against the wetlands beyond.

PRISMATIC SETTING

Glass Block, Solar-Reflective & Laminated Glass

Even though architect **Edward R. Niles** is not interested in reiterating the past, this "all-glass" oceanfront home has the type of purity deemed "classic" throughout the ages.

The technologically demanding siting necessitated a structural combination of concrete caissons and rigid steel frame. The steel wedge is supported by a grid of concrete caissons embedded six feet into the volcanic substrate. All vertical and seismic loads are transferred through the diagonal wedge frame, rigid frames and horizontal steel and concrete diaphragm.

Having achieved such structural support, Niles was free to use an infinity of glass, and he did. Nothing seems to exist between the interior and the elements as each plane of glass acts in unison with the weather and its constantly changing energy and light.

A great space to freely experience nature, the house itself feels like a wave — the primal sun and sea its source of light, sound and color.

Photography by Alan Weintraub

RIGHT & BELOW RIGHT *To make the most of a three-bedroom home's oceanfront location, Edward Niles and architect **James Corcoran** used an enormity of double-glazed, green-tinted solar-reflective glass. The south and west facing glass allows unobstructed views of the beach and the Channel Islands beyond, while glass block on the north side gives privacy from the street.*

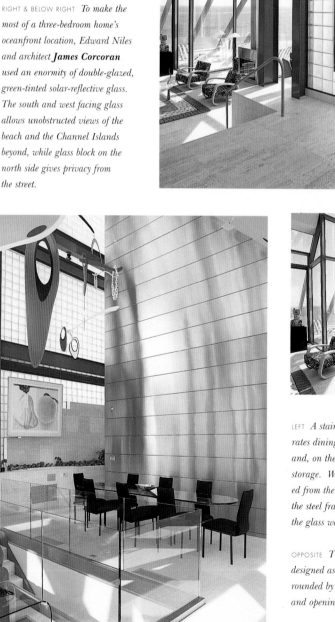

LEFT *A stainless steel tower separates dining and kitchen areas and, on the kitchen side, provides storage. Works of art are suspended from the ceiling or supported by the steel frames that float beyond the glass walls.*

OPPOSITE *The living area is designed as one great platform surrounded by glass and glass block and opening onto the terrace.*

STRUCTURAL ENGINEER: *David Weiss*
MECHANICAL ENGINEER: *American Energy Consultants*
GENERAL CONTRACTOR: *Robert Walter*
DOUBLE-GLAZED, GREEN-TINTED SOLAR-REFLECTIVE GLASS: *Center Glass*
GLASS BLOCK: *Bob Whitham*
LAMINATED GLASS (RAILING): *Pittsburgh Corning Corporation*

INNER PEACE

Glass Block

Deep in a canyon, the home of Dr. Paul Miller and his wife Peggy Nazarey is buttressed from the intrusive technology of contemporary Los Angeles by architect **Steven Ehrlich's** serenely private architecture which opens outward toward the ruggedly natural site.

From the entry's soothing sound of a splashing waterfall, to the central three-story glass block atrium bisecting the house, to the living areas' shoji screens and glass walls that slide open to dissolve all boundaries between indoors and out, light and space are linked inextricably. The effect of transmitted and reflected light is a remarkably transcendent peace. Or what would you call seeing hummingbirds in silhouette through your living room walls?

GLASS BLOCK: *Pittsburgh Corning Corporation*

RIGHT *A stairway cantilevered directly from the atrium wall, to which it is anchored to a steel frame within, is exposed in the architect's celebration of structure.*

Photography by Christopher Dow

ABOVE *When closed, the living room's shoji screens substitute for glass as a diffuser of light, casting sunbeams and shadows.*

ABOVE RIGHT *As does glass block, the rice paper shoji screens continue the light play day and night.*

RIGHT *Bridges of Plexiglas joined with steel link the home's two distinct parts with an airy transparency. The steel monument frame provides stability against Los Angeles' prevalent earthquakes, and while it would have been easier and less costly to conceal them, the architect chose to expose the steel beams in salute to the precision with which they have been crafted to frame the glass block walls.*

When the shoji screens are open, the white oak floors continue the role of reflecting light and all boundaries between indoors and out are dissolved.

A GLEAMING PALETTE

Tempered Glass, Laminated Plate Glass, Cast Glass, Sandblasted Glass,
Dichroic Glass, Mirror & Prisms

The extensive use of glass throughout this contemporary version of an Italian villa overlooking Seattle's Lake Washington seems particularly appropriate. Its owner, a prominent art patron, is a trustee of the Seattle Art Museum and one of the founders of the nearby Pilchuck Glass School, the nation's most noted school of its kind and which has helped forge the Northwest's leadership in art glass. In designing the house, Olson/Sundberg Architects' **Jim Olson** and **Tom Kundig** viewed glass as an "episodic" material that they consciously wove through the house in ways both common and extraordinary.

Working with interior designer **Mary Siebert**, the architects created spaces that would be large enough to accommodate the client's collection as well as several artworks specifically commissioned for the home. In addition, the idea of organizing the structure like an Italian Renaissance villa, with grand public spaces on the main level and smaller ones upstairs, prompted the use of warm Italianate colors as well. The light palette, combined with the reflective poetry of glass used not only structurally but also as a predominant material by the artists represented in the collection, is remarkably hospitable.

LEFT *The hue of the home's exterior stucco establishes the light palette continued within, working with the predominating glass, used structurally and also for individual works of art, to create an invitingly warm reflectivity throughout.*

BELOW *Greeting visitors at the entry is a vertical glass art screen, approximately four-feet-by-six-feet, created in collaboration between glass artists Jamie Carpenter and Dale Chihuly. The round balloon-shaped work in glass at right is by the late Christopher Willmarth.*

Photography by Michael Jensen

LAMINATED GLASS: *Libbey Owens Ford Co.*
TEMPERED GLASS (GUARDRAILS): *Libbey Owens Ford Co.*
COLORED GLASS (USED FOR DALE CHIHULY'S ARTWORKS THROUGHOUT):
Olympic Color Rods

The architects worked directly with Stanislav Libensky from the Czech Republic who created this work in cast-lead glass for the reflecting pool.

OPPOSITE *A glowing fireplace surround fills the sitting room with a soft translucence. The surround is made of standard glass with a lightly sandblasted interior surface that is floated one inch from a painted wall. The metal-framed fireplace opening stands away from the glass to allow the flames' reflections to be diffused outward and upward through the glass.*

FAR RIGHT *Glass art continues to take center stage in the master bath. Illuminated by a skylight beyond the marble tub enclosure are vases by Dante Marioni and a warrior head by Charles Parriott.*

RIGHT *For one display area, the architects used standard sheet glass that is simply scored and snapped to shape. The edges have been lightly polished and stacked flat.*

The color, depth and fascinating play of glass art itself sparks virtually every wall and horizontal space. Major pieces creating the glistening interplay are by such artists as **Dale Chihuly, Ed Carpenter, Stanislav Libensky, Cappy Thompson, Jamie Carpenter, Dante Marioni, Charles Parriott, Marvin Lipofsky, Ginny Ruffner, William Morris** and the late **Christopher Willmarth**.

Perhaps the most unusual of the commissioned pieces and certainly the most complex is Ed Carpenter's skylight over the central stair. Working closely with the architects, the architectural glass artist responded to their desire for a house that would become more ethereal as one ascends. With the side of the skylight well splayed outward at fifteen degrees and mirrored, the stairwell appears to open directly to the heavens. The cantilevered sculptural wings of glass which emerge through the mirrored surfaces float illusively above as one goes upstairs, refracting and reflecting images of clouds, sun and stars.

The effect of such luminous works by Carpenter and the others within these Tuscan-inspired spaces is an unfolding panorama of nature's own glories transformed by dreams.

LEFT *The bay window provides a glass envelope through which to look out toward Mount Rainier and also on which to mount a changing display of art. All windows in the home are laminated glass to filter out ultraviolet light, which damages fragile art, custom rugs and furniture. Most glass used is standard clear, which actually has a slightly green cast. Metal overhangs both provide shade from direct sunlight and obscure the line between inside and outside.*

LEFT *The dining room, as all areas of the home, is arranged so that furniture, when not being used otherwise, can host displays of the client's collection. Here on the buffet, right to left, are works in glass by Dale Chihuly, Marvin Lipofsky, Stanislav Libensky, Ginny Ruffner, Harvey Littleton and William Morris. On the wall at right is Abstract Screen, a 1961 collage by Paul Horiuchi. The horse is by Deborah Butterfield.*

OPPOSITE *A large wall at the landing was kept blank to act as a canvas for the commissioned glass skylight by Ed Carpenter. Slowly transforming light paintings are projected onto the wall after dark by a bank of computerized lights which shine from the roof down through the sculpture. Materials used are: 8 mm Asahi Opal Glass 80, a luminous blue glass that transmits a sunshine-yellow light and which is laminated to three-eighth-inch clear plate glass, and dichroic glass, ribbed plate glass, beveled glass and prisms laminated to the plate glass.*

RIGHT *The refracted light of Ed Carpenter's prismatic skylight floods the stairwell with a warm brilliance, at the same time enhancing works of art such as the Mayan stele in the foreground.*

RIGHT *The cast glass vanity designed by the architects is actually fused glass using standard glass chips that are baked in a mold for an extended period of time. The mirror light is also made of glass that has been fused into flat plate glass, but crystal-clear rather than standard glass was used so that there would be no green cast. The stained glass is by Cappy Thompson.*

GAME OF ILLUSIONS

Mirror

This apartment in Rome measures just 950 square feet, but Transit Design's **Gianni Ascarelli, Maurizio Macciocchi** and **Danilo Parisio** have made it seem without end. Prohibited by the city's strict building codes from making the desired physical changes, the architects used full-height mirrored panels to transform the space visually instead.

RIGHT *In the entry, mirrored doors projecting into the space and framed with pediments begin the illusionary game.*

Photography by Giovanna Piemonti

ABOVE & OPPOSITE *Nineteenth-century antiques are juxtaposed with contemporary platforms for seating and storage. Some doors slide open, others swing open, and some face each other, creating "halls of mirrors" that seem to go on forever.*

LEFT *The glass-topped Mizar table, designed by Superstudio for Cristal Art in the 1970s, seems created specifically to accompany the obelisk-shaped cabinetry designed by Transit.*

WRAPAROUND GLAMOUR

Tempered Glass

The grandeur of the spaces in a classical contemporary Houston residence designed by Lloyd Jones Fillpot Associates Architects demanded an entry that would harmonize both function and aesthetics with equal distinction. Interior designer **Erika Brunson** and her associate, architect **David Speaks**, not only equalled but enhanced it through a combination of glass and polished brass that became a significant exterior as well as interior feature through its lofty sublimity.

Glass combined with limestone, marble, brass and bronze provides a glamorous welcome to this home in Texas. The entry doors are made of brass grids inset with panels of half-inch-thick clear glass with a hand-ground bevel on both sides and along all edges. The wraparound wall is made of curved clear glass held in place with bronze medallions with flush silicon glazing.

Photography courtesy of Erika Brunson Design Associates

BRINGING MEMORIES TO LIGHT

Stained & Beveled Glass

" Light ... transparency ... reflection ... distortion ... magic ... poetry. Glass is much more than just a useful material, it has to do with feelings and memories, mystery and mysticism," says **Gerard Pascal**, who, with his brother **Carlos Pascal**, uses glass throughout the homes they design to interact with light and fill them with soul.

RIGHT *Based on a window in Frank Lloyd Wright's Dana House, this leaded stained glass elevates the atmosphere of a home in Mexico City.*

BELOW & OPPOSITE *In another living room in Mexico City, art deco style doors and skylight establish a mood of elegance.*

Photography by Eitan Feinholz

OPENING UP A TUDOR

Tempered Glass

"Open" and "Tudor" seem contradictory terms, yet the enclosed rear deck that completed the renovation of this Tudor-style home in Fort Worth, Texas, made it extremely open and livable without sacrificing the classic feeling of its Old World theme.

Interior designer *Joseph Minton*, working in collaboration with architect *Robert H. LeMond*, created the atrium to enable his client and lifelong friend to enjoy a spectacular view day or night. In this transparent but safe haven, even electrical storms can be a source of enjoyable entertainment.

Twenty-four-foot ceilings allow the enclosed rear deck to open onto both the first floor living room and dining room as well as the second-floor master bedroom and sitting room. A reflective coating added to the inside of the glass ceiling provides ultraviolet protection and reduces heat gain.

Photography by Emily Minton

PALLADIAN SYMMETRY

Tempered Glass

Inspired by the harmonious balance in Andrea Palladio's classical Roman style when she added a window to this Honolulu home, **Allison Holland** considered the effect on the entire structure. The result not only opened up what previously was a dark and dismal hallway, but also, when viewed from without, enhances the property's sense of total symmetry.

PALLADIAN WINDOW: *Pella Corporation*
CONSERVATORY: *Amdega Machin Conservatories*

RIGHT & BELOW LEFT *The elegance the new window brings to the exterior is repeated inside, inviting Hawaii's strong natural light to illuminate the birds, branches and flowers in the handpainted mural by Charles R. Gracie & Son, Inc., the design of which is repeated in the sheer lace drapery. By removing an interior wall separating the stairs and replacing it with a Chippendale-style bannister, and by exposing the garden through the window, the designer has added a sense of much breadth to the narrow hallway.*

Photography by David Livingston

BELOW & OPPOSITE *To balance the existing structure's glass conservatory, which is used as a kitchen, Allison Holland added a similarly vertical, curved and white-trimmed feature, a graceful, sixteen-foot-high Palladian window, on the home's opposite side.*

A HELLENISTIC WELCOME

Laminated, Sandblasted, Tempered & Triple-Glazed, Insulated Security Glass & Mirror

Often the ideal place to look for design inspiration is within one's own home. The illustrations in a cherished book, the colors in a favorite scarf, the craftsmanship of a loved one's hand-me-down. When architect **Lee Harris Pomeroy** wanted to create a pair of curved, etched glass entry doors for the library he designed for his wife Sarah, a noted classics scholar and author, he based his design on two Hellenic women depicted in a book she had written.

Making the library the home's pièce de résistance was an appropriate note for this home, a grand old turn-of-the-century

RIGHT *Circular glass windows respond to the historic architecture of the turn-of-the-century building.*

Photography throughout by Paul Warchol

RIGHT & OPPOSITE *To fabricate these elegant door panels, blown-up photographs of two ancient Greek terra-cotta figurines were transposed to an interlayer and then permanently encapsulated between two clear sheets of bent safety glass. Cesar Color's ChromaFusion is a high-tech photo-imaging and enlargement process by which any image in any color can be produced on the firm's proprietary interlayer material. The result looks like traditional sandblasted glass and is particularly suitable when a sleek rather than rough or porous surface is desired. The custom mahogany door frame was made by Robert Soule, New Haven, Connecticut.*

Photography right by Tom Berntsen

GLASS PANELS: *Cesar Color Inc.*
TEMPERED GLASS (RAILING): *American Glass Company*
GLASS DOORS: *Duratherm Window Corporation*
GREENHOUSE WINDOW: *American Storefront Company*
MIRROR: *American Glass Company*
SECURITY GLASS AND GREENHOUSE ROOF: *American Storefront Company*

The triple-glazed, insulated
security glass and greenhouse roof
permit a two-level ficus tree to
grow within a New York City
penthouse. The window wall
opens to a planted terrace,
designed to balance the views of
Central Park on the opposite side
of the living room.

apartment house in New York City overlooking Central Park West. Its turrets, copper mansard roof and dormer windows looking out to the park and the Guggenheim Museum, which is directly opposite the penthouse, suggest a time for study and repose. From the greenhouse roof at the entry, which permits a ficus to grow alongside a harpsichord in the adjacent living room, to the reading terrace outside the upper floor of the two-level library that is located in the building's corner turret, being at home with education and the arts is a feeling carried throughout.

LEFT *This second-story guest bathroom features a greenhouse wall of windows facing west and located above a whirlpool bathtub. The mirror is a combination of sandblasted and mirrored surfaces.*

ABOVE *Dormer windows cut within the copper mansard roof reveal copper decorative elements from the window below. This creates a dramatic double frame for the Central Park view. It is framed first by the window and then by the historic copper element on the outside.*

169

The glass doors open to the reading terrace from the upper floor of the two-level library, which is located in the building's corner turret. Glass railings surrounding the terrace provide safety as well as protection from gusty winds.

The library's two levels are connected by a metal staircase, curved in conformity to the turret and appearing to wrap around a circular glass oculus set into the floor of the topmost space.

G L O S S A R Y

Edited from information supplied by the
Glass Association of North America
3310 S.W. Harrison Street
Topeka, Kansas 66611-2279

Acid Polishing   The polishing of a glass surface by acid treatment.

Annealing   The process of preventing objectionable stresses in glass during manufacture by controlling cooling. Re-annealing is the process of removing objectionable stresses in glass by re-heating to a suitable temperature followed by controlled cooling.

Anti-Walk Blocks   Rubber blocks that prevent glass from moving sideways in the glazing rabbet from thermal effects or vibration.

Art Glass   Colored translucent glass, often called art glass, opalescent glass, cathedral glass or stained glass, is produced by the rolling process but generally in small, batch-type operations. There are usually variegated colors within each sheet produced, and no two sheets will match for hue. Thickness will vary within a sheet as well as from sheet to sheet. The maximum thickness produced is usually one-eighth inch. When used as a glazing material, Art Glass should be glazed in the same manner as tinted/heat-absorbing glass. Art glass cannot be heat-strengthened or tempered.

Autoclave   A vessel that employs high pressure and heat. In the glass industry, used to produce a bond between glass and PVB (polyvinyl butyral) or urethane sheet.

Back Putty   (See "Bed")

Back-up   A material placed into a joint, primarily to control the depth of the sealant and to prevent adhesion at the base of the sealant bead.

Batter   A surface defect that looks like hammered metal. Unless very heavy, it usually cannot be seen by the naked eye, although it is clearly seen on the shadowgraph. (See "Shadowgraph")

Bead   A sealant after application in a joint irrespective of the method of application, such as caulking bead and glazing bead. Also a molding or stop used to hold glass or panels in positions.

Bed or Bedding   In glazing, the bead of compound applied between a lite of glass or panel and the stationary stop or sight bar of the sash or frame. It is usually the first bead of a compound to be applied when setting glass or panels. (See "Back Putty")

Bedding of Stop   In glazing, the application of compound at the base of the channel, just before the stop is placed in position, or buttered on the inside face of the stop. (See "Buttering")

Bent Glass   Flat glass that has been shaped while hot into cylindrical or other curved shapes.

Bevel of Compound Bead   In glazing, a bead of compound applied to provide a slanted top surface so that water will drain away from the glass or panel.

Beveling   The process of edge-finishing flat glass to a bevel angle.

Bite   Amount of overlap between the stop and the panel or lite.

Blisters   Relatively large bubbles or gaseous inclusions in the glass. (Extremely small gaseous inclusions are called "seeds.") Except from the standpoint of appearance, seeds and blisters are usually quite harmless.

Block   A small piece of lead, rubber or other suitable material used to position the glass in the frame.

Bloom   A surface film on glass resulting from attack by the atmosphere, or by deposition of smoke or other vapors.

Bow   A continuous curve of the sheet, either vertical or horizontal.

Bronze Glass   A glare and heat-reducing glass which is intended for applications where glare control and reduction of solar heat is desired or where color can contribute to design.

Brush Lines   Fine parallel surface lines having the general appearance of brush marks in paint. Also called "end lines."

Bubbles   Gaseous inclusions in glass, normally brilliant in appearance.

Bulb Edge   In float glass manufacture, the extreme lateral edge of the ribbon as drawn.

Bullet Resisting Glass   A multiple lamination of glass with tough, clear, sheet plastic, usually at least one-and-three-sixteenth-inch thick overall, which is designed to stop bullets from ordinary firearms other than high-powered rifles.

Buttering   Application of sealant compound to the flat surface of some member before placing the member in position, such as the buttering of a removable stop before fastening the stop in place.

Carved Glass   Glass that is carved to various depths by sandblasting to create embossed/relief/textural effects.

Casting   Shaping glass by pouring it into or on molds, tables or rolls.

Cathedral Glass   (See "Art Glass")

Channel   A three-sided, U-shaped opening in sash or frame to receive lite or panel, as with sash or frame units in which the lite or panel is retained by a removable stop. Contrasted to a rabbet, which is a two-sided L-shaped opening, as with faced glazed window sash.

Checks (Vents)   Very small cracks in flat glass, usually at the edge. Though small, these are cause for concern since they can be intensified under strain.

Chemical Durability   The lasting quality, both physical and chemical, of a glass surface. It is frequently evaluated after prolonged weathering or storage, in terms of physical and chemical changes in the glass surface. (See "Weathering")

Chipped Edge   An imperfection due to breakage of a small fragment from the cut edge of the glass. Generally this is not serious except in heat-absorbing glass.

Clips   Wire spring devices to hold glass in rabbeted sash, without stops, and face glazed.

Compound   A formulation of ingredients, usually grouped as vehicle or polymer pigment and fillers to produce caulking compound, elastomeric joint sealant, etc.

Compression   Pressure exerted on a sealant in a joint, as by placing a lite or panel in place against bedding, or placing a stop in position against a bead of sealant.

Consistency   Degree of softness or firmness of a compound as supplied in the container and varying according to method of application, such as gun, knife, tool, etc.

Chord   Measurement for bent glass representing the distance straight across the curve from point to point.

Cords   Attenuated glassy inclusions that possess optical and other properties differing from those of the surrounding glass. Cords are the result of non-homogeneity. Low-intensity cords are called "strings" or "wire lines."

Crush   A lightly pitted area resulting in a dull gray appearance over the region.

Cullet   Broken glass, excess glass from a previous melt, or edges trimmed off when cutting glass to size. Cullet, in some regular proportion, is an essential ingredient in the raw batch charge in glass-making in that it facilitates melting.

Curing Agent   One part of a two-part sealant which, when added to the base, will cause the base to change its physical state by chemical reaction between the two parts.

Cut Sizes   Glass ordered with width and length specified, and not as stock sheets. Cut sizes are furnished with sizes guaranteed to be cut to at least the dimensional tolerances stipulated.

Cutter   One who cuts flat glass. Also, the tool used in cutting glass.

Cutting   Scoring flat glass with a diamond or a steel or hard alloy wheel and breaking it along the score.

Decolorizer   Material or agent used in the batch to remove color, or to decolorize glass.

Decolorizing   The process of producing a colorless appearance in glass.

Devitrification   Crystallization in glass.

Dice   The more or less cubical pattern of fracture of fully tempered glass, the edges of the dice being roughly equal to the thickness of the glass.

Diffusing   Scattering, dispersing, as the tendency to eliminate a direct beam of light.

Digs   Deep, short scratches.

Dirt   A small particle of foreign matter imbedded in the glass surface.

Distortion   The characteristic surface waviness of glass. It is often confused with "brush lines" and "end lines" but is not at all related. Seldom met within an objectionable degree, it can be evaluated on the shadowgraph.

Double Glazed   Two panes of glass installed with an intervening air space. The glass may be pre-assembled into a unit (i.e., insulating glass) or may be two separate panes.

Double Strength   In float glass, approximately one-eighth-inch thick.

Dry Seal   Accomplishment of weather seal between glass and sash by use of Neoprene (or other flexible material) strips or gaskets. A dry seal may not be completely watertight.

Edging   Grinding the edge of flat glass to a desired shape or finish.

Elastomer   An elastic, rubber-like substance, such as natural or synthetic rubber.

Emissivity   The ability of a material to emit radiant energy. Emittance is the ratio of the total radiant energy emitted by a given surface to that emitted by an ideal black body at the same temperature. To emit is to give out, to discharge -- in the case of glass, essentially, to reradiate absorbed energy (heat).

Etch   To attack the surface of glass with hydrofluoric acid or other agent, generally for marking or decoration.

Exterior Glazed   Glass set from the exterior of the building.

Exterior Stop   The removable molding or bead that holds the lite or panel when it is on the exterior side of the lite or panel, as contrasted to an interior stop located on the interior side of the lite.

Face Glazing   On rabbeted sash without stops, the triangular bead of compound applied with a glazing knife after bedding, setting and clipping the lite in place.

Figured Glass   Rolled glass having a patterned or figured surface. Most patterns can be obtained with one side smooth fire-polished (i.e., "as rolled"). Some patterns are available with both surfaces figured.

Fire-Polish   To make glass smooth or glossy by the action of fire.

Flat Ground Edge   Edge ground flat and perpendicular to the glass surface.

Flare   A protrusion on the edge of a lite of glass due to improper cutting.

Flat Glass   A general term that embraces float glass and various forms of rolled glass (as contrasted with fiberglass, containers, etc.).

Float Glass   Glass drawn over a bath of molten tin to attain a fire polish.

Front Putty   In glazing, the putty forming a triangular fillet between the surface of the glass and the front edge of the rabbet.

Frosted Finish   A surface treatment for glass, consisting of an acid-etching of one or both surfaces that improves distribution of transmitted light and reduces glare.

Fully Tempered Glass   Glass that has been tempered to a high degree. Fully tempered glass, if broken, will disintegrate into many small pieces (dice) which are more or less cubical. Fully tempered glass is four to five times stronger than annealed glass of the same thickness.

Gaseous Inclusions   Round or elongated bubbles in the glass.

Gaskets   Preformed shapes, such as strips and grommets, of rubber or rubber-like composition, used to fill and seal a joint or opening either alone or in conjunction with a supplemental application of a sealant.

Gauge   To measure the thickness of flat glass. Also, refers to the thickness of the glass.

Glass   An inorganic product of fusion which has cooled to a rigid condition without crystallizing. It is typically hard and brittle and has a conchoidal fracture. It may be colorless or colored, and transparent to opaque. Masses or bodies of glass may be made colored, translucent or opaque by the presence of dissolved, amorphous or crystalline material.

Glazing   The securing of glass in prepared openings in windows, door panels, partitions, etc.

Glazing Quality   In float glass, this represents the usual selection supplied when quality is not otherwise definitely specified.

Gray Glass   (See "Bronze Glass")

Gun Consistency   Sealant formulated in a degree of softness suitable for application through the nozzle of a caulking gun.

Heat-Absorbing Glass   Glass for intercepting appreciable portions of radiant energy, especially solar energy. It is obtainable as float or patterned glass. Heat-absorbing glass is made in only one quality in type of glass. (See "Bronze" and "Gray Glass")

Heat-Resisting Glass   Glass able to withstand high thermal shock, generally because of low coefficient of expansion.

Heat-Strengthened Glass   Glass that has been heat-treated to a state less than that of fully tempered glass. Heat-strengthened glass is not considered a safety glass and will not completely dice as will fully tempered glass.

Heat-Treated Glass   Term sometimes used for both fully tempered glass and heat-strengthened glass.

Heel Bead   Sealant applied at the base of channel, after setting lite or panel and before the removable stop is installed, as one of its purposes is to prevent leakage past the stop.

High-Transmission Glass   Glass which transmits an exceptionally high percentage of visible light.

Imperfections   The tempering process rarely introduces imperfections into glass. The basic glass may contain bubbles, vents, chips and inclusions which, if accepted or not revealed by inspection before tempering, can cause breakage in the initial heating or final quench operations. If inclusions are not eliminated by self-destruction during the tempering process, in rare cases they may lead to failure at a later time.

Insulating Glass Units   Most insulating glass units consist of two panes of glass enclosing a hermetically sealed air space. The panes are held apart by a spacer around the entire perimeter. The spacer contains a moisture-absorbent material, called a desiccant, that serves to keep the enclosed air free of visible moisture. The entire perimeter of the assembly is sealed with an organic sealant.

Interior Glazed   Glass set from the interior of a building.

Interior Stop   The removable molding or bead that holds the lite in place, when it is on the interior side of the lite, as contrasted to an exterior stop which is located on the exterior side of a light or panel.

Interlayer   A layer of standard or polycarbonate-compatible polyvinyl butyral or of urethane used to bind two or more pieces of glass or glass-and-polycarbonate sheet into a laminated unit.

Iridescence   (See "Strain Pattern")

Kiln Formed Glass   Glass with a textural relief caused by heating flat glass in a kiln over a mold.

Kink   Similar to a warp, but of shorter distance between high and low points of deviation from plane. Usually associated with vertically tempered glass.

Knife Consistency   Compound formulated in a degree of firmness suitable for application with a glazing knife such as used for face glazing and other sealant applications.

Knot   An imperfection in glass. An inhomogeneity in the form of a vitreous lump.

Laminate   A composite unit of glass and interlayer material.

Laminated Glass   A combination of two or more lites of glass with a layer of tough, transparent vinyl between glass forming a single construction. When laminated glass is fractured, the particles of glass tend to adhere to the plastic, affording protection against flying or falling particles.

Lehr   A long, tunnel-shaped oven for annealing or reannealing glass, usually by continuous passage.

Light   (see "Lite")

Lime Glass   The most commonly melted form of clear, uncolored flat glass, so called because a principal ingredient, besides sand, is lime (CaO).

Lines   (See "Brush Lines" and "Cords")

Lite   Another term for a pane of glass used in a window. Sometimes spelled "light" in the industry literature, but spelled "lite" in this text to avoid confusion with light as "visible light."

Low-E or Low Emissivity Glass or other materials which have a low rate of emitting (radiating) absorbed radiant energy. The radiant energy (heat) is, in effect, reradiated back toward its source.

Mastic Descriptive of heavy-consistency compounds that may remain adhesive and pliable with age.

Mirror Virtually all mirrors for interior use are manufactured by the wet deposition method. Silver, then copper, is deposited from solutions onto the wet glass by chemical reaction. The glass is then dried and the copper is painted. (See also "Two-Way (Transparent) Mirror")

Mitered Edge Flat edge ground at an angle (other than 90 degrees) to the glass surfaces.

Monolithic A glazing assembly consisting of only one lite or pane of glass, polycarbonate, acrylic or plastic.

Non-Drying Descriptive of a compound that does not form a surface skin after application.

One-Way (First Surface) Mirror A mirror produced by deposition of reflective metal on the front surface of glass, usually under vacuum.

Opalescent Glass (See "Art Glass")

Patterned Glass (Also "Rolled" or "Rough Rolled Glass") One type of rolled glass having a pattern impressed on one or both sides. Used extensively for light control and decorative glazing.

Plate Glass Manufactured by the grinding and polishing process. In the United States it is no longer produced and has been replaced by the float glass process.

Ply A single layer of glass or interlayer.

Points Thin, flat, triangular or diamond-shaped pieces of zinc used to hold glass in wood sash by driving them into the wood.

Polariscope A device for examining the degree of strain in a sample of glass.

Polished Edge An edge finish, smooth and nearly equal to the luster on the face of the glass.

Polished Wire Glass Wired glass that has been ground and polished on both surfaces.

Polyvinyl Butyral (PVB) Viscoelastic plasticized thermoplastic film commonly used as the interlayer for laminated glass.

Priming Sealing of a porous surface so that compound will not stain, lose elasticity or shrink excessively because of loss of oil or vehicle into the surround. A sealant primer or surface conditioner may be used to promote adhesion of a curing type sealant to certain surfaces.

Processed Glass Glass in which the surface has been altered by processes such as etching, sandblasting, chipping, grinding and ceramic-enameling, to change its light diffusion or to give decorative effects. Either or both surfaces may be so treated. Also, glass which has been further treated after forming, such as edge work, tempering and staining.

Rabbet A two-sided L-shaped recess in sash or frame to receive lites or panels. When no stop or molding is added, such rabbets are face glazed. Addition of a removable stop produces a three-sided U-shaped channel.

Reflective Glass
Glass with a reflective surface film to reduce heat and light transmission.

Retrofit Reflective Films Organic coatings or reflective films can be applied to existing in-place glass to reduce excessive solar heat gain or glare. These are generally a flow-on acrylic plastic, or a tinted or metalized polyester, adhesive-coated film. These coatings not only reflect but also absorb solar energy.

Roll Impressions (Also "Roll Distortions") Indentations in the surface of rolled glass, with or without an asbestos mark in the center, that are caused by contact of the glass with the rolls and/or displaced roll disks while the set is in a plastic state.

Roll Marks (Also "Roll Scratches") A series of the fine parallel scratches or tears on the surface of rolled glass in the direction of draw. They are one-eighth inch long or smaller, but usually so fine and so close together that they appear to be a series of incipient checks rather than scratches. They are caused by a difference in velocity between rolls and the sheet of glass.

Rolled Glass Glass formed by rolling, including patterned and wired glass. As the glass is drawn horizontally from the tank, figured, engraved, etched machine rolls impress a pattern on the surface of the glass, varying from almost smooth to deeply marked geometric, fluted or random overall designs. It is made in thicknesses from one-eighth to three-eighths inch.

Rub (Also "Crush") A series of small scratches in glass generally caused during transport by a chip lodged between two lites.

Safety Glass Glass so constructed, treated or combined with other materials as to reduce, in comparison with ordinary sheet glass, float glass, rolled glass or plate glass, the likelihood of cutting and piercing injury to persons by these safety glasses should they be broken by human contact. Fully tempered glass is a safety glass.

Sandblasted Finish A surface treatment for flat glass obtained by spraying the glass with hard particles so as to clip out and roughen one or both surfaces of the glass. The effect is to increase obscurity and diffusion, but it also makes the glass fragile and hard to clean.

Sash The frame, including muntin bars when used, and including the rabbets to receive lites of glass, either with or without removable stops, and designed either for face glazing or channel glazing.

Sawcut Edge Glass edge-cut with a carbide- or diamond-tipped saw usually at a right angle to the glass surfaces.

Scratches Any marking or tearing of the surface appearing as though it had been done by either a sharp or rough instrument.

Screw-On Bead or Stop Stop, molding or bead fastened by machine screws as compared with those that snap into position without additional fastening.

Sculptured Glass Works assembled for their own intrinsic value incorporating glass crafted by the use of various techniques.

Sealant Compound used to fill and seal a joint or opening, as contrasted to a sealer which is a liquid used to seal a porous surface.

Seam To grind, usually with an abrasive belt, wet or dry, the sharp edges of a piece of glass. Also called "swipe."

Seamed Edge Glass edge which has been chamfered at the intersection of the glass surfaces and the cut edge.

Seeds Minute bubbles less than 1/32 inch in diameter. Fine seeds are visible only upon close inspection, usually appearing as small specks, and are an inherent defect in the best quality of float glass.

Setting Placement of lites or panels in sash or frames. Also action of a compound as it becomes more firm after application.

Shading Coefficient Total solar heat gain (directly transmitted radiation plus portion of absorbed radiation that enters the building) for the specified glass or glass-and-shading combination divided by the total solar heat gain for one-eighth-inch clear glass.

Shadowgraph A device for examining glass with respect to distortion, batter and lines, although other defects are also prominently revealed.

Shelf Life Used in the glazing and sealant business as referring to the length of time a product may be stored before beginning to lose its effectiveness. Manufacturers usually state the shelf life and the necessary storage conditions on the package.

Slip Sheet The interleaving paper placed between lites of glass in a package to protect them from scratching and fading (also called "paper-packed").

Smoke Streaked areas appearing as slight discoloration.

Solarization Change in transmission, and sometimes of color, of glass as a result of exposure to sunlight or other radiation.

Solar-Reflective Glass Glass with a mirror-like metallic or metallic-oxide coating that is highly reflective of solar energy. In addition, major attributes include the aesthetic appeal of the variously colored reflective coatings (silver, gold, copper and blue that can then be combined with clear, bronze, gray, green and blue float glass), as well as energy savings and occupant comfort.

Spacers (Shims) Small blocks of composition board or other material placed on either side of lites or panels to center them in the channel and maintain uniform width of sealant beads. Prevent excessive sealant distortion.

Spandrel Glass Glass used in non-vision areas of a structure or curtainwall. The glass has been either fully tempered or heat strengthened to develop physical properties which materially increase its resistance to breakage from wind load and the thermal stresses induced by temperature difference.

Stain Attack of a glass surface by water or other solutions involving: leaching of sodium ions to the surface of the glass; an increase in pH on the glass surface; the breaking of silica bonds in the glass structure. If this process advances to the last stage, the glass will have a blotched, streaked and cloudy appearance and cannot be restored to pristine condition short of grinding and polishing the damage away, a process that is generally more expensive than simply replacing the glass.

Stained Glass (See "Art Glass")

Stationary Stop   The permanent stop or lip of a rabbet on the side away from the side on which lites or panels are set.

Stones   Crystalline contaminations in the glass, usually pieces of undissolved or crystallized silica, bits of refractory, or crystals due to devitrification. Stones are detrimental to appearance and may seriously weaken the glass, particularly if present in highly stressed areas.

Stop   Either the stationary lip at the back of a rabbet, or the removable molding at the front of the rabbet, either or both serving to hold lite or panel in sash or frame, with the help of spacers.

Strain Pattern   Elastic deformation due to stress. The tempering process places glass under very high compression on the surface and high tension in the core of the glass. This results in a specific geometric optical pattern in the glass which is not normally visible, but which may become apparent under certain conditions of illumination, especially when light is polarized, such as in a skylight or other forms of reflected light. The colors of the strain pattern are sometimes referred to as iridescent, or the general condition as iridescence. The pattern that is seen under certain lighting conditions may vary with each manufacturer, depending on the design of the cooling apparatus. Strain pattern is characteristic of all fully tempered glass.

Stress   Any condition of tension or compression existing within the glass, particularly due to incomplete annealing, temperature gradient or inhomogeneity.

String   Transparent lines appearing as though a thread of glass has been incorporated into the sheet.

Structural Silicone Glazing   Based on the use of a silicone sealant not only as a weather seal but also for the structural transfer of loads from the glazing panel to its perimeter support system. Certain specific silicone sealant formulations are the only sealants, to date, found to be suitable for this purpose.

Tempered Glass   Glass that has been rapidly cooled from near the softening point, under rigorous control, to increase its mechanical and thermal endurance. Fully tempered glass always dices into a multitude of small particles.

Thermal Endurance   The relative ability of glass to withstand thermal shock.

Tinted Glass   Glass with a material added to give the glass a light and/or heat-reducing capability and color.

Tongless Tempered
Refers to glass that is tempered, using a support method other than tongs, resulting in a product without tong marks.

Tong Marks
Small surface indentations near and parallel to one edge of vertically tempered or heat-strengthened glass resulting from the tongs used to suspend the glass during the heat treating process.

Transmittance
The ability of the glass to transmit solar energy in the visible light, the ultraviolet, and infrared ranges, centrally measured in percentages of each.

Two-Way (Transparent) Mirror   A one-way mirror on which an additional thin film of reflective coating has been deposited. Designed to allow vision from one direction while presenting a mirror appearance from the opposite side. Light intensity on the viewer's side of the mirror should be significantly less than on the subject's side, enabling the viewer to see through the mirror as through a transparent glass, while preventing the subject looking at the mirror from seeing the viewer.

Unit   Term normally used to refer to one single assembly of insulating glass.

Urethane   Flexible thermoplastic interlayer compatible with polycarbonate, acrylic and glass.

Vinyl Glazing   Holding glass in place with extruded vinyl channel or roll-in type.

Warp   The easily seen undulate deviation of the sheet from a plane surface. Microscopic deviation would be "distortion" or "batter." (See "kink")

Wave   An optical effect due to uneven glass distribution or low-intensity cords.

Weathering (Also "Stain")   Attack of a glass surface by atmospheric elements. (See "Chemical Durability")

Weeps (Weep Holes)   Drain holes in the sash to prevent water accumulation from condensation, rain and cleaning.

Wet Seal   Application of an elastomeric sealant between the glass and sash to form a weathertight seal.

Wired Glass, Flat   Rolled glass having a layer of meshed or stranded wire completely embedded as nearly as possible to the center of thickness of the sheet. This glass is obtainable as polished glass (one or both surfaces) and patterned glass. Approved wired glass is used as transparent or translucent fire-retardant glazing, and sometimes as decorative glass or as security glazing. It breaks more easily than unwired glass of the same thickness, but the wire restrains the fragments from falling out of the frame when broken.

DIRECTORY

ARCHITECTS, DESIGNERS & ARTISTS

Ronald W. Aarons, AIA
Aarons & Associates
23875 Ventura Boulevard #203B
Calabasas, California 91302
United States
Tel: (818) 222-1600
Fax: (818) 591-9052

Reginald Adams
Reginald Adams & Associates
8500 Melrose Avenue, Suite 207
Los Angeles, California 90069
United States
Tel: (310) 659-8038
Fax: (310) 659-8594

Franco Audrito
Studio 65
Via Po 14
10123 Torino
Italy
Tel: (39) 11 839 5691
Fax: (39) 11 812 5592

Jeffrey Bishop
84 Forsyth Street, #7
New York, New York 10002
United States
Tel: (212) 925-1434

James Blakeley III, ASID
Blakeley-Bazeley Ltd.
Post Office Box 5173
Beverly Hills, California 90210
United States
Tel: (213) 653-3548
Fax: (213) 653-3550

Joseph Braswell, ASID
Joseph Braswell & Associates
425 East 58th Street, #26E
New York, New York 10022
United States
Tel: (212) 688-1075
Fax: (212) 752-7167

W. Douglas Breidenbach, AIA, Architect
1925 Montana Avenue, Suite 2
Santa Monica, California 90402
United States
Tel/Fax: (310) 576-7915

Erika Brunson Design Associates
Erika Brunson
David Speaks
903 Westbourne Drive
Los Angeles, California 90069
United States
Tel: (310) 652-1970
Fax: (310) 652-2381

Ed Carpenter
1812 N.W. 24th Avenue
Portland, Oregon 97210
United States
Tel/Fax: (503) 224-6729

Jamie Carpenter
145 Hudson Street, Fourth Floor
New York, New York 10013
United States
Tel: (212) 431-4318
Fax: (212) 431-4425

Warren Carther
Carther Studio Inc.
464 Hargrave Street
Winnipeg, Manitoba R3A OX5
Canada
Tel: (204) 956-1615
Fax: (204) 453-2496

Dale Chihuly
509 North East Northlake Way
Seattle, Washington 98105
United States
Tel: (206) 632-8707
Fax: (206) 632-8825

Carl D'Aquino Interiors, Inc.
Carl D'Aquino
Paul Laird
Geordi Humphreys
Jaime Vasquez
520 Broadway, Room 701
New York, New York 10012
United States
Tel: (212) 925-1770
Fax: (212) 431-0771

Alfredo De Vido, FAIA
Alfredo De Vido Associates
1044 Madison Avenue
New York, New York 10028
United States
Tel: (212) 517-6100
Fax: (212) 517-6103

Steven Ehrlich, FAIA
Steven Ehrlich Architects
2210 Colorado Avenue
Santa Monica, California 90404
United States
Tel: (310) 828-6700
Fax: (310) 828-7710

Rand Elliott, FAIA
Elliott + Associates Architects
6709 North Classen, Suite 101
Oklahoma City, Oklahoma 73116
United States
Tel: (405) 843-9554
Fax: (405) 843-9607

Peter Forbes & Associates, Inc.
Peter Forbes, AIA
Gerard A. Gutierrez
Barry Dallas
Bradford C. Walker, AIA
70 Long Wharf
Boston, Massachusetts 02110
United States
Tel: (617) 523-5800
Fax: (617) 523-5810

Ron Goldman, FAIA
Goldman/Firth/Boccato
24955 Pacific Coast Highway, Suite A202
Malibu, California 90265
United States
Tel: (310) 456-1831
Fax: (310)456-7690

H. Theodore Graves, AIA
H.T. Graves & Associates
71 Arch Street
Greenwich, Connecticut 06830
United States
Tel: (203) 661-1011

J. Kevin Gray
Kevin Gray Design
1000 West Avenue
Miami Beach, Florida 33139
United States
Tel: (305) 531-6908
Fax: (305) 531-0771

Joan Gray
Grayson Interior Design
266 Post Road East
Westport, Connecticut 06880
United States
Tel: (203) 222-7661
Fax: (203) 221-8263

Christian Grimonprez
Zuidstraat 42
8800 Roeselare
Belgium
Tel: (32) 57 240091
Fax: (32) 57 241423

Hanrahan & Meyers, Architects
Thomas Hanrahan
Victoria Meyers
One Union Square West, Suite 506
New York, New York 10003
United States
Tel: (212) 989-6026
Fax: (212) 255-3776

Meryl Hare, MSIDA, MDIA
Hare & Klein Pty Ltd.
11 Chuter Street
McMahons Point, Sydney, New South Wales 2060
Australia
Tel: (61) 2 954 0461
Fax: (61) 2 955 4896

Jean-Pierre Heim, Architect DPLG
Jean-Pierre Heim & Associates
24, rue Vieille du Temple
75004 Paris
France
Tel: (33) 1 4278 0815
Fax: (33) 1 4277 0181
ALSO:
140 West 69th Street, 46B
New York, New York 10023
United States
Tel: (212) 724-7132
Fax: (212) 724-7943

Margaret Helfand Architects
Margaret Helfand
Marti Cowan
32 East 38th Street
New York, New York 10016
United States
Tel: (212) 779-7260
Fax: (212) 779-7758

Donald C. Hensman, FAIA
Buff, Smith & Hensman
1450 West Colorado Boulevard
Pasadena, California 91105
United States
Tel: (818) 795-6464
Fax: (818) 795-0961

Agustin Hernandez, Arquitecto
Bosques de Acacilas, #61
Col. Bosques de Las Lomas
Mexico 10 D.F. C.P. 11700
Tel: (525) 596 1154
Fax: (525) 596 1710

David Hertz, AIA
Syndesis, Inc.
2908 Colorado Avenue
Santa Monica, California 90404-3616
United States
Tel: (310) 829-9932
Fax: (310) 829-5641

Allison Holland, ASID
Creative Decorating
168 Poloke Place
Honolulu, Hawaii 96822
United States
Tel: (808) 955-1465
Fax: (808) 949-2290

Hugh Newell Jacobsen, FAIA, Architect
Hugh Newell Jacobsen, FAIA
Thérèse Baron Gurney, ASID
2529 P Street, N.W.
Washington, D.C. 20007
United States
Tel: (202) 337-5200
Fax: (202) 337-3609

Perry Janke
225 North Michigan Avenue, Suite 800
Chicago, Illinois 60601
United States
Tel: (312) 938-4455
Fax: (312) 938-0929

Dennis Jenkins Associates
Dennis Jenkins, ASID, IIDA
Kim Rizio
Laura Barrett
5813 Southwest 68th Street
South Miami, Florida 33143
United States
Tel: (305) 665-6960
Fax: (305) 573-1744

Brian E. Kaye
David McAlpin Architect PC
160 Fifth Avenue, Suite 901
New York, New York 10010-7003
United States
Tel: (212) 929-3883
Fax: (212) 633-0078

Tom Kundig
Olson/Sundberg Architects
108 First Avenue South
Seattle, Washington 98104
United States
Tel: (206) 624-5670
Fax: (206) 624-3730

Kari Kuosma Architects
　　　Kari Kalevi Kuosma
　　　Esko Valkama
Vainamöisenkatu 21 A 3
00100 Helsinki
Finland
Tel: (358) 0 447677
Fax: (358) 0 447679

Anne Leepson
Grayson Construction, Inc.
266 Post Road East
Westport, Connecticut 06880
United States
Tel: (203) 221-7426
Fax: (203) 221-8263

Robert H. LeMond
LeMond Associates Architects
3508 Park Hill Drive
Fort Worth, Texas 76109
United States
Tel: (817) 926-3433
Fax: (817) 924-8768

Stanislav Libensky
Zelezny Brod
Pelechovna 645
46822 Czech Republic
Tel: (42) 3 287 2340
Fax: (42) 2 287 4132

Marvin Lipofsky
Pilchuck Glass School
1201 316th Street, N.W.
Stanwood, Washington 98292
United States
Tel: (360) 445-3111
Fax: (360) 445-5515

Christine Maclin
Christine Maclin Interior Design
723 Congress Street
Portland, Maine 04102
United States
Tel: (207) 774-9545
Fax: (207) 871-0117

Dante Marioni
4136 Meridian Aveune, North
Seattle, Washington 98103
United States
Tel: (206) 282-7971
Fax: (206) 632-1363

Nancy Mee
6202 37th Avenue, N.E.
Seattle, Washington 98115
United States
Tel: (206) 525-1922
Fax: (206) 524-6619

Joseph Minton
Joseph Minton, Inc.
3320 West Seventh Street
Fort Worth, Texas 76107
United States
Tel: (817) 332-3111
Fax: (817) 429-6111

Juan Montoya
Juan Montoya Design
80 Eighth Avenue
New York, New York 10011
United States
Tel: (212) 242-3622
Fax: (212) 242-3742

William Morris
William Morris Studio
31321 Third Avenue, N.E.
Stanwood, Washington 98292
United States
Tel: (360) 445-3111
Fax: (360) 445-5515

Edward R. Niles, Architect
　　　Edward R. Niles, FAIA
　　　James Corcoran, Architect
　　　Lisa Niles McCarthy, Architect
29350 Pacific Coast Highway, # 9
Malibu, California 90265
United States
Tel: (310) 457-3602
Fax: (310) 457-3376

Jim Olson
Olson/Sundberg Architects
108 First Avenue, South
Seattle, Washington 98104
United States
Tel: (206) 624-5670
Fax: (206) 624-3730

Charles Parriott
Pilchuck Glass School
1201 316th Street, N.W.
Stanwood, Washington 98292
United States
Tel: (360) 445-3111
Fax: (360) 445-5515

Pascal Arquitectos
　　　Carlos Pascal
　　　Gerard Pascal
Atlaltunco 99,
Tecamachalco Edo de Mexico
C.P. 53950 Mexico
Tel: (525) 294 2371
Fax: (525) 294 8513

Lee Harris Pomeroy, AIA
Lee Harris Pomeroy Associates
462 Broadway, Third Floor
New York, New York 10013
United States
Tel: (212) 334-2600
Fax: (212) 334-0093

Powell/Kleinschmidt
　　　Donald D. Powell
　　　Robert D. Kleinschmidt
645 North Michigan Avenue, Suite 810
Chicago, Illinois 60611
United States
Tel: (312) 642-6450
Fax: (312) 642-5135

Bart Prince, Architect
3501 Monte Vista, N.E.
Albuquerque, New Mexico 87106
United States
Tel: (505) 256-1961
Fax: (505) 268-9045

Christopher Rebman
Christopher Rebman International Design Group
4100 Massachusetts Avenue, N.W., Suite 107
Washington, D.C. 20016
United States
Tel: (202) 364-0820
Fax: (202) 364-8081

Ginny Ruffner
1306 Western Avenue, #403
Seattle, Washington 98101
United States
Tel: (206) 587-2323
Fax: (206) 343-9592

Sheri Schlesinger
Schlesinger & Associates
101 South Robertson Boulevard, Suite 202
Los Angeles, California 90048
United States
Tel: (310) 275-1330
Fax: (310) 275-8698

Louis Shuster
Shuster Design Associates, Inc.
1401 East Broward Boulevard, Suite 103
Ft. Lauderdale, Florida 33301
United States
Tel: (305) 462-6400
Fax: (305) 462-6408

Mary Siebert
Siebert & Associates
1415 Second Avenue South
Seattle, Washington 98101
United States
Tel/Fax: (206) 621-7676

Angelo Tartaglia, Architect
Via Boezio, 92/D9A
00192 Rome
Italy
Tel: (39) 6 687 3879
Fax: (39) 6 686 8449

Cappy Thompson
707 South Snoqualmie, #4A
Seattle, Washington 98108-1700
United States
Tel/Fax: (206) 292-9592

Transit Design
　　　Gianni Ascarelli
　　　Maurizio Macciocchi
　　　Danilo Parisio
Via Emilio Morosini, 17
00153 Rome
Itlay
Tel: (39) 6 589 9848
Fax: (39) 6 589 8431

Aldo Vandini
Koaladesign, srl
via Belle Arti, 8
40126 Bologna
Itlay
Tel: (39) 51 224 747
Fax: (39) 51 263 786

David Walker, Architect
85 Seaforth Crescent
Seaforth, New South Wales
Australia
Tel: (61) 2 948 7958
Fax: (61) 2 948 7652

Gary Whitfield, Architect
Whitfield Associates
1100 South Coast Highway, Suite 201
Laguna Beach, California 92651
United States
Tel: (714) 497-5466
Fax: (714) 497-3481

Robert Whitfield, Architect
516 East Paces Ferry Road
Atlanta, Georgia 30305
United States
Tel: (404) 266-8344
Fax: (404) 237-6932

Christopher Willmarth
Deceased

James P. Wright
Venice Atelier Architects
645 Oxford Avenue
Venice, California 90291
United States
Tel/Fax: (310) 305-1179

MANUFACTURERS & SUPPLIERS

Dennis Abbe
246 West End Avenue
New York, New York 10023
United States
Tel: (212) 787-3851

A.C.I. Distributing
9010 South Norwalk Boulevard
Santa Fe Springs, California 91350
United States
Tel: (800) 774-4224
Fax: (818) 506-3836

Acralight
2491 Dubridge
Irvine, California 92714
United States
Tel: (800) 325-4355
Fax: (714) 863-0324

Alpana Aluminum Products
2915 Niagara Lane North
Plymouth, Minnesota 55447
United States
Tel: (612) 478-6313
Fax: (612) 478-6804

AMA Glass Corporation
970 West 190th Street, Suite 603
Torrance, California 90502
United States
Tel: (310) 327-1414
Fax: (310) 327-0110

Amdega Machin Conservatories
Post Office Box 7
Glenview, Illinois 60025
United States
Tel: (708) 729-7212
Fax: (708) 729-7214

American Energy Consultants
8444 Melba Avenue
Canoga Park, California 91305
United States
Tel/Fax: (818) 346-7240

American Glass Company
132-15 Northern Boulevard
Flushing, New York 11354
United States
Tel: (718) 939-4749
Fax: (718) 463-8894

American Storefront Company
132-15 Northern Boulevard
Flushing, New York 11354
United States
Tel: (718) 939-4749
Fax: (718) 463-8894

Andersen Corporation
100 Fourth Avenue North
Bayport, Minnesota 55003-9989
United States
Tel: (800) 426-7691
Fax: (612) 439-5150

Arcadia Manufacturing Inc.
Post Office Box 416
New Canaan, Connecticut 06840
United States
Tel: (800) 423-6565

Arte & Vetro
Mrs. Boettega
Via Cibrario 50
Turin
Italy
Tel: (39) 11 489759

Asahi Glass Company Limited
1-2, Marunouchi 2-chome
Chiyoda-ku
Tokyo 100
Japan
Tel: (81) 3 3218 5313
Fax: (81) 3 3213 1358

Atlanta Glasscrafters
3888 Flowers Road
Atlanta, Georgia 30360
United States
Tel: (404) 451-4835
Fax: (404) 451-4838

Bischoff Studios, Inc.
Route 2, Box 230
Quincy, Florida 32351
United States
Tel: (904) 875-3184
Fax: (904) 875-4184

Bizazza s.p.a.
36041 Alte-Vicenza
Itlay
Tel: (39) 444 490833
Fax: (39) 444 696174

Blomberg Window Systems
1453 Blair Avenue
Post Office Box 22485
Sacramento, California 95822-0485
United States
Tel: (916) 428-8060
Fax: (916) 422-1967

Bourke & Mathews
Post Office Box 1304
New Canaan, Connecticut 06840
United States
Tel: (203) 622-0576
Fax: (914) 273-9548

Greyson Bryan
35857 Beach Road
Capistrano Beach, California 92624
United States
Tel: (714) 240-4778
Fax: (714) 240-0712

Burt Lockhart/Jerry Fulks and Company
210 Third Avenue South, #400
Seattle, Washington 98104
United States
Tel: (206) 624-5509
Fax: (206) 624-2925

Carmel Architectural Sales
1173 North Armando Street
Anaheim, California 92806
United States
Tel: (714) 630-7221
Fax: (714) 630-0668

Center Glass
1433 Arundel Avenue
Ventura, California 93003
United States
Tel: (805) 642-0419
Fax: (805) 642-8421

Cesar Color Inc.
880 Hinckley Road
Burlingame, California 94010
United States
Tel: (415) 259-9700
Fax: (415) 259-0701

Cherry Creek
3500 Blake Street
Denver, Colorado 80205
United States
Tel: (303) 295-1010
Fax: (303) 295-1161

Collier Building Specialties
1485 Bayshore Boulevard, #153
San Francisco, California 94124
United States
Tel: (415) 467-9235
Fax: (415) 468-4796

Coughlin Builders
14431 Ventura Boulevard, #407
Sherman Oaks, California 91423
United States
Tel: (818) 905-1637
Fax: (818) 501-4325

D.B.I.
Zone Industrielle Tournai Ouest
Rue de L'Ancienne Potence 18
7501 Orcq
Belgium
Tel: (32) 69 234 882
Fax: (32) 69 842 314

Dee's Glass
110 West Spazier Avenue
Burbank, California 91502
United States
Tel: (213) 849-3427
Fax: (213) 849-3479

John Depp
41-40 38th Street
Long Island City, New York 11101
United States
Tel: (718) 784-8500
Fax: (718) 784-9018

Design Supply
1861 North Topanga Canyon Boulevard, Suite H
Topanga Canyon, California 90290
United States
Tel: (310) 455-3132
Fax: (310) 455-1062

Dimensions in Glass
142 Kings Highway
Fairfield, Connecticut 06430
United States
Tel: (203) 367-1888
Fax: (203) 368-1888

Dlubak Corporation
904 Freeport Road
Freeport, Pennsylvania 16229
United States
Tel: (412) 295-5167
Fax: (412) 295-989

Dunstone Maze Pty Ltd.
21 Garema Court
Kingsgrove, New South Wales
Australia
Tel: (61) 2 740 4444
Fax: (61) 2 740 4392

Duratherm Window Corporation
RR1, Box 945
North Vassalborro, Maine 04962
United States
Tel: (207) 872-5558
Fax: (207) 872-6731

Exquisite Glass & Stone, Inc.
123 Allen Street
New York, New York 10002
United States
Tel: (212) 674-7069
Fax: (212) 473-4808

Farallon Studios, Inc.
Post Office Box 835
Sausalito, California 94965
United States
Tel: (415) 332-2222
Fax: (415) 332-7624

Fidenza Vetraria s.p.a.
Via S. Felice Casati, #32
20121 Milan
Italy

Fleetwood Aluminum
2485 Railroad
Corona, California 91720
United States
Tel: (800) 736-7363
Fax: (714) 279-8068

Flickinger Glassworks, Inc.
204-207 Van Dyke Street
Pier 41
Brooklyn, New York 12231
United States
Tel: (718) 875-1531
Fax: (718) 875-4264

Gramar Industries
116 East 16th Street, Ninth Floor
New York, New York 10003
United States
Tel: (516) 599-3605
Fax: (516) 593-8376

Guillaume Saalburg
70 rue Jean Bleuren
Vannes
France
Tel: (33) 1 4638 7676
Fax: (33) 1 4638 7400

Kevin Harper
Southwest Construction Service
21722 Esmalte
Mission Viejo, California 92692
United States
Tel: (714) 855-1504
Fax: (714) 830-2954

J & M Manufacturing
Post Office Box 3606
Vista, California 92085
United States
Tel: (619) 591-9972
Fax: (619) 591-9255

Kalwall
1111 Candia Road
Post Office Box 237
Manchester, New Hampshire 03105
United States
Tel: (603) 627-3861
Fax: (603) 627-7905

Karl Springer Ltd.
306 East 61st Street
New York, New York 10021
United States
Tel: (212) 752-1695
Fax: (212) 644-3023

Harold Lehr
112 Green Street
Greenpoint, New York 11222
United States
Tel: (914) 569-8860
Fax: (914) 569-8890

Libbey-Owens-Ford
Post Office Box 799
Toledo, Ohio 43697
United States
Tel: (419) 247-4721
Fax: (419) 247-4517

Louis Baldinger & Sons
19-02 Steinway Street
Astoria, New York 11105
United States
Tel: (718) 204-5700
Fax: (718) 721-4986

Malibu Glass & Mirror
Gerald Lemonnier
3547 Winter Canyon
Malibu, California 90265
United States
Tel: (310) 456-1844
Fax: (310) 456-2594

Mark Hill Fabrications Inc.
359 South Mountain Road
Gilboa, New York 12079
United States
Tel: (607) 588-9403
Fax: (607) 588-6825

Marvin Windows
Post Office Box 100
Warroad, Minnesota 56763
United States
Tel: (218) 386-1430
Fax: (218) 386-3906

Metal Window Corp.
501 South Isis Avenue
Inglewood, California 90301
United States
Tel: 213) 776-1383
Fax: (310) 641-7356

The Meyne Company
Division of Bulley & Andrews
1755 West Armitage Avenue
Chicago, Illinois 60622
United States
Tel: (312) 207-2100
Fax: (312) 207-0488

Mirage Vinyl Doors & Windows
11651 Vanowen Street
North Hollywood, California 91605
United States
Tel: (818) 765-5666
Fax: (818) 765-6336

Modu-Line Windows
930 Single Avenue
Wassau, Wisconsin 54403
United States
Tel: (800) 521-8742
Fax: (715) 842-3281

Morrow & Morrow Corporation
426 Georgina Avenue
Santa Monica, California 90402
United States
Tel: (310) 394-1021
Fax: (310) 394-0579

Nemo Tile
48 East 21st Street
New York, New York 10010
United States
Tel: (212) 505-0009

North Fulton Glass
281 South Atlanta Street
Roswell, Georgia 30075
United States
Tel: (404) 992-5308
Fax: (404) 641-1894

Olympic Color Rods
2020 124th Avenue, N.E.
Bellevue, Washington 98027
United States
Tel: (800) 445-7742
Fax: (206) 861-7386

Pacific Skylights
2491 Dubridge
Irvine, California 92714
United States
Tel: (714) 863-9343
Faz: (714) 863-0324

Parenti & Raffaelli
215 East Prospect Avenue
Mount Prospect, Illinois 60056
United States
Tel: (708) 253-5550
Fax: (708) 253-6055

Pella Corporation
102 Main Street
Pella, Iowa 50219
United States
Tel: (515) 628-1000
Fax: (515)628-6070

Pella of Georgia
2030 Powers Ferry Road, Suite 217
Atlanta, Georgia 30339
United States
Tel: 404) 850-8600
Fax: (404) 850-9630

Pittsburgh Corning Corp.
800 Presque Isle Drive
Pittsburgh, Pennsylvania 15239
United States
Tel: (412) 327-6100
Fax: (412) 327-5890

Polytronix, Inc.
805 Alpha Drive
Richardson, Texas 75081
United States
Tel: (214) 238-7045
Fax: (214) 644-0805

Project Team Alphen aan den rijn B.V.
Postbus 172
2400 AD Alphen A/D Rijn
The Netherlands
Tel: (31) 17 203 9948
Fax: (31) 17 202 2454

Rambusch
40 West 13th Street
New York, New York 10011
United States
Tel: (212) 675-0400
Fax: (212) 620-4687

Ken Renwick
Post Office Box 877
Laguna Beach, California 92652
United States
Tel: (714) 499-0123

S.A. Bendheim, Inc.
61 Willett Street
Passaic, New Jersey 07055
United States
Tel: (201) 471-1733
Fax: (201) 471-3475

Saint Gobain
Via Romagnoli, 6
20146 Milan
Italy
Tel: (39) 24 243 211
Fax: (39) 24 954 045

Saint-Roch
Zone Industrielle de Florette 5150
Belgium
Tel: (32) 81 449 411
Fax: (32) 81 449 450

SGO Glassworks
1827 North Case Street
Orange, California 92665
United States
Tel: (714) 974-6124
Fax: (714) 974-6529

Shading Systems Inc.
Post Office Box 5697
Clark, New Jersey 07066-5697
United States
Tel: (800) 255-5988
Fax: (908) 688-5575

Skydome Pty Ltd.
Queens Road
Five Dock, New South Wales
Australia
Tel: (61) 2 745 1522
Fax: (61) 2 744 1268

Stamford Iron and Steel
Post Office Box 2190
Glenbrook, Connecticut 06906
United States
Tel: (203) 324-6751
Fax: (203) 324-9130

Sundial-Schwartz, Inc.
159 East 118th Street
New York, New York 10035
United States
Tel: (212) 289-4969
Fax: (212) 996-3236

Sunglow Skylight Products
3124 Gillham Plaza
Kansas City, Missouri 64109
United States
Tel: (816) 561-1155
Fax: (816) 561-5327

Ron Taybi
31252 Ceanothus Drive
Laguna Beach, California 92651
United States
Tel: (714) 499-2243
Fax: (714) 540-3231

Tempwerks
2901 Saco Street
Vernon, California 90058
United States
Tel: (213) 846-1565
Fax: (213) 846-1569

Terry Sash and Door
3250 San Fernando Road
Los Angeles, California 90065
United States
Tel: (213) 478-2290
Fax: (213) 478-2291

T.M. Cobb
Ventana Distributing
1921 Gates Avenue, Suite A
Redondo Beach, California 90278
United States
Tel/Fax: (310) 372-5065

Trilogy Glass Design
8137 Remmet Avenue
Canoga Park, California 90304
United States
Tel: (818) 716-1068
Fax: (818) 716-0715

UltraGlas, Inc.
9186 Independence Avenue
Chatsworth, California 91311
United States
Tel: (818) 722-7744
Fax: (818) 722-8231

U.S. Aluminum Corporation
3663 Bandini Boulevard
Vernon, California 90023
United States
Tel: (800) 766-6063
Fax: (800) 866-6063

Dimitry Vergun
1546 Seventh Street, Suite 101
Santa Monica, California 90401
United States
Tel: (310) 458-9919
Fax: (310) 458-1435

Vetreria Corticella Felsinia srl.
Via del Carrozzaio, 6
Bologna
Itlay
Tel: (39) 51 530 105
Fax: (39) 51 535 640

Robert Walter
R.R. Walter Co.
1645 Pacific Avenue, Suite 104
Oxnard, California 93033
United States
Tel: (805) 483-3199
Fax: (805) 483-5842

David Weiss
David Weiss Structural Engineer
22440 Clarendon Street, Suite 203
Woodland Hills, California 91367
United States
Tel: (818) 224-3973
Fax: (818) 224-3922

PHOTOGRAPHERS

Jaime Ardiles-Arce
730 Fifth Avenue
New York, New York 10019
United States
Tel: (212) 333-8779
Fax: (212) 593-2070

Peter Aarons/ESTO
ESTO Photographers
222 Valley Place
Mamaroneck, New York 10543
United States
Tel: (914) 698-4060
Fax: (914) 698-1033

Tom Bernsten
180 Varick Street 5th Floor
New York, New York 10014
United States
Tel: (212) 255-6210
Fax: (212) 255-6107

Tom Bonner
1201 Abbot Kinney
Venice, California 90251
United States
Tel: (310) 396-7125

Nike Bourgeois
Zuidstraat 42
8800 Roeselare
Belgium
Tel: (32) 57 24 2423
Fax: (32) 57 24 7423

Dick Busher
7042 20th Place N.E.
Seattle, Washington 98115
United States
Tel: (206) 523-1426

Frederick Charles
254 Park Avenue South
Studio 7F
New York, New York 10010
United States
Tel: (212) 505-0686
Fax: (212) 505-0692

Christopher Covey
664 North Madison Avenue
Pasadena, California 91101
United States
Tel: (818) 440-0284

Billy Cunningham
26 St. Mark's Place, Apt. 4FW
New York, New York 10003
United States
Tel: (212) 677-4904

Edoardo D'Antona
Via Montesamtor
00195 Rome
Italy
Tel: (39) 6 370 1411

Christopher Dow
1016 Alta Pine Drive
Altadena, California 91001
United States
Tel: (800) 910-7937

Eitan Feinholz
Atlatunco-#99
Tecamachalco
Mexico 53970
Tel: (525) 294 23 71
Fax: (525) 294 85 13

Jane Gottlieb
544 Dryad Road
Santa Monica, California 90402
United States
Tel: (310) 573-1515
Fax: (310) 573-1558

Janos Grapow
Via Monti Parioli 21/A
Rome
Italy
Tel: (39) 06 32 44 831

John Hall
885 Tenth Avenue
New York, New York 10019
United States
Tel: (212) 757-0369

Alec Hamer
626 East 20th Street
New York, New York 10009
United States
Tel: (212) 353-1988

Hedrich-Blessing
11 West Illinois Street
Chicago, Illinois 60610
Unites States
Tel: (312) 321-1151
Fax: (312) 321-1165

Douglas Hill
2324 Moreno Drive
Los Angeles, California 90039
United States
Tel: (213) 660-0681

Michael Jensen
665 Northwest 76th Street
Seattle, Washington 98117
United States
Tel: (206) 789-7963

Foster Karicofe
1901 Laguna Canyon Road, Suite #1
Laguna Beach, California 92651
United States
Tel: (714) 494-1656

Robert C. Lautman
4906 41st Street North West
Washington, D.C. 20016
United States
Tel: (202) 966-2800
Fax: (202) 362-7483

David Livingston
1036 Erica Road
Mill Valley, California 94941
United States
Tel: (419) 383-0898
Fax: (419) 383-0892

Jon Miller
Hedrich-Blessing
11 West Illinois Street
Chicago, Illinois 60610
United States
Tel: (312) 321-1151
Fax: (312) 321-1165

Emily Minton
3004 13th Avenue Suite #1
Birmingham, Alabama 35209
United States
Tel: (205) 332-4888

George Mott
51 Bank Street
New York, New York 10014
United States
Tel: (212) 242-2753

Mary E. Nichols
Mary E. Nichols Photography
132 South Beachwood Drive
Los Angeles, California 90004
United States
Tel: (213) 935-3080
Fax: (213) 935-9788

Anthony Peres
645 Oxford Avenue
Venice, California 90291
United States
Tel/Fax: (310) 821-1984

Matteo Piazza
Studia 65
Viapo 14
Torino
Italy

Giovanna Piemonti
Via della Pilotte 21/Q
Rome
Italy
Tel: (39) 6 573 00419

Undine Prohl
1930 Ocean Avenue #302
Santa Monica, California 90405
United States
Tel/Fax: (310) 399-5031

Marvin Rand
1310 Abbot Kinney Boulevard
Venice, California 90291
United States
Tel: (310) 936-3441
Fax: (310) 396-2366

Al Rosenberg
60 Ambassador Drive
Winnipeg, Manitoba
Canada
Tel: (204) 338-0710
Fax: (204) 338-0840

Claudio Santini
29500 Heather Cliff Road #17
Malibu, California 90265
United States
Tel: (310) 457-7978
Fax: (310) 457-1364

Kim Sargent
Sargent Photography
1235 U.S. Highway One
Juno Beach, Florida 33408
United States
Tel: (407) 627-4711
Fax: (407) 694-9078

Bob Shimer
Hedrich-Blessing
11 West Illinois Street
Chicago, Illinois 60610
United States
Tel: (312) 321-1151
Fax: (312) 321-1165

Michael Ian Shopenn
Post Office Box 1141
Port Townsend, Washington 98368
United States
Tel: (360) 385-1276
Fax: (360) 385-4874

Steinkamp/Ballogg, Chicago
666 West Hubbard Street
Chicago, Illinois 60610
United States
Tel: (312) 421-1233

Tim Street-Porter
2075 Watsonia Terrace
Los Angeles, California 90068
United States
Tel: (213) 874-4278

Jussi Tianen
Limingantie 40
Dossohelsinki
Finland
Tel: (358) 0 798 876

Deidi von Schaewen
12, rue Popincourt
75011 Paris
France
Tel: (331) 48 064 972
Fax: (331) 48 064 623

Paul Warchol
Paul Warchol Photography
133 Mulberry Street-#6S
New York, New York 10013
United States
Tel: (212) 431-3461
Fax: (212) 274-1953

Richard Waugh
9A Alpha Road
Willoughby NSIV 2068
Australia
Tel/Fax: (02) 958-7425

Alan Weintraub
Alan Weintraub Photography
1832A Mason Street
San Francisco, California 94133
United States
Tel: (415) 553-8191
Fax: (415) 553-8192

INDEX

ARCHITECTS, DESIGNERS AND ARTISTS

A
Aarons, Ronald W. *134-139*
Adams, Reginald *106-107*
Ascarelli, Gianni *156-157*
Audrito, Franco *62-63*

B
Barrett, Laura *36-37*
Bishop, Jeffrey *88-93*
Blakeley, James III *84-85*
Braswell, Joseph *94-97*
Breidenbach, W. Douglas *42-43, 76-79*
Brunson, Erika *158-159*
Buff, Smith & Hensman *80-81*

C
Carpenter, Ed *150-155*
Carpenter, Jamie *150-155*
Carther, Warren *126-127*
Chihuly, Dale *150-155*
Corcoran, James *144-145*
Cowan, Marti *124-125*

D
Dallas, Barry *68-73*
D'Aquino, Carl *108-113*
De Vido, Alfredo *54-57*

E
Ehrlich, Steven *146-149*
Elliott, Rand *140-143*

F
Forbes, Peter *68-73*

G
Goldman, Ron *18-23*
Graves, Ted *140-143*
Gray, J. Kevin *118-119*
Gray, Joan *32-35*
Grimonprez, Christian *120-123*
Gurney, Thérèse Baron *14-17*
Gutierrez, Gerard A. *68-73*

H
Hanrahan, Thomas *114-117*
Hare, Meryl *44-47*
Heim, Jean-Pierre *98-99*
Helfand, Margaret *124-125*
Hensman, Donald C. *80-81*
Hernandez, Agustin *82-83*
Hertz, David *128-131*
Holland, Allison *164-165*
Humphreys, Geordi *108-113*

J
Jacobsen, Hugh Newell *14-17*
Janke, Perry *60-61*
Jenkins, Dennis *36-37*

K
Kaye, Brian E. *118-119*
Kleinschmidt, Robert D. *104-105*
Kundig, Tom *150-155*
Kuosma, Kari Kalevi *50-53*

L
Laird, Paul *108-113*
Leepson, Anne *32-35*
LeMond, Robert H. *162-163*
Libensky, Stanislav *150-155*
Lipofsky, Marvin *150-155*

M
Macciocchi, Maurizio *156-157*
Maclin, Christine *68-73*
Marioni, Dante *150-155*
McCarthy, Lisa Niles *24-29*
Mee, Nancy *88-93*
Meyers, Victoria *114-117*
Minton, Joseph *162-163*
Montoya, Juan *30-31*
Morris, William *150-155*

N
Niles, Edward R. *24-29, 144-145*

O
Olson, Jim *88-93, 150-155*

P
Parisio, Danilo *156-157*
Parriott, Charles *150-155*
Pascal, Carlos *160-161*
Pascal, Gerard *160-161*
Pomeroy, Lee Harris *166-171*
Powell, Donald D. *104-105*
Prince, Bart *38-39*

R
Rebman, Christopher *62-63*
Rizio, Kim *36-37*
Ruffner, Ginny *150-155*

S
Schlesinger, Sheri *80-81*
Shuster, Louis *64-67*
Siebert, Mary *150-155*
Speaks, David *158-159*

T
Tartaglia, Angelo *58-59*
Thompson, Cappy *150-155*
Transit Design *156-157*

V
Valkama, Esko *50-53*
Vandini, Aldo *100-103*
Vasquez, Jaime *108-113*

W
Walker, Bradford C. *68-73*
Walker, David *44-47*
Whitfield, Gary *40-41*
Whitfield, Robert *64-67*
Willmarth, Christopher *150-155*
Wright, James P. *74-75*

MANUFACTURERS, SUPPLIERS AND ARTISANS

A
Abbe, Dennis *108-113*
A.C.I. Distributing *18-23*
Acralight *76-79*
Alpana Aluminum Products Inc. *60-61*
AMA Glass Corporation *128-131*
Amdega Machin Conservatories *164-165*
American Energy Consultants *24-29, 144-145*
American Glass *68-73*
American Glass Company *166-171*
American Storefront Company *166-171*
Andersen Corp. *40-41*
Arcadia Manufacturing Inc. *68-73*
Arte & Vetro *62-63*
Asahi Glass Company Limited *128-131*
Atelier Guillaume Saalburg *98-99*
Atlanta Glasscrafters *64-67*

B
Bischoff Studios *36-37*
Bizazza s.p.a. *118-119, 124-125*
Blomberg Window Systems *74-75*
Bourke & Mathews *140-143*
Bryan, Greyson *40-41*
Burt Lockhart/Jerry Fulks and Company *88-93*

C
Carmel Architectural Sales *18-23, 24-29*
Center Glass *144-145*
Cesar Color Inc. *60-61, 166-171*
Cherry Creek *108-113*
Collier Building Specialties *74-75*
Coughlin Builders *134-139*

D
D.B.I. *120-123*
Dee's Glass *24-29*
Depp, John *30-31*
Design Supply *42-43*
Dimensions in Glass *32-35*
Dlubak Corporation *108-113*
Dunstone Maze Pty Ltd. *44-47*
Duratherm Window Corporation *166-171*

E
Exquisite Glass & Stone, Inc. *114-117*

F
Farallon Studios, Inc. *64-67*
Fidenza Vetraria s.p.a. *58-59*
Fleetwood Aluminum *134-139*
Flickinger Glassworks, Inc. *114-117*

G
Gramar Industries *118-119*

H

Harper, Kevin *40-41*

J

J & M Manufacturing *42-43*

K

Kalwall *18-23, 24-29, 74-75*
Karl Springer Ltd. *94-97*

L

Lehr, Harold *124-125*
Libbey-Owens-Ford *18-23, 68-73, 150-155*
Lohja/Uniplast/Finland *50-53*
Louis Baldinger & Sons *94-97*

M

Malibu Glass & Mirror/Gerald Lemonnier
    18-23
Mark Hill Fabrications Inc. *124-125*
Marvin Windows *32-35*
Metal Window Corp. *18-23*
Meyne Company, The *60-61*
Mirage Vinyl Doors & Windows *76-79*
Modu-Line Windows *68-73*
Morrow & Morrow Corporation *42-43*

N

Nemo Tile *118-119, 124-125*
North Fulton Glass *64-67*

O

Olympic Color Rods *150-155*

P

Pacific Skylights *134-139*
Parenti & Raffaelli *104-105*
Pella Corporation *164-165*
Pella of Georgia *64-67*
Pittsburgh Corning Corp. *24-29, 40-41, 128-131,*
    144-145, 146-149
Polytronix, Inc. *18-23*
Project Team Alphen aan den rijn B.V. *14-17*

R

Rambusch *108-113*
Renwick, Ken *40-41*

S

S.A. Bendheim, Inc. *108-113*
Saint Gobain *58-59, 100-103*
Saint-Roch *120-123*
SGO Glassworks *36-37*
Shading Systems Inc. *118-119*
Sisco *68-73*
Skydome Pty Ltd. *44-47*
Stamford Iron and Steel *140-143*
Sundial-Schwartz, Inc. *94-97*
Sunglow Skylight Products *64-67*

T

Taybi, Ron *40-41*
Tempwerks *128-131*
Terry Sash and Door *134-139*
T.M. Cobb/Ventana Distributing *76-79*
Trilogy Glass Design *106-107*

U

UltraGlas, Inc. *84-85*
U.S. Aluminum Corporation *18-23*

V

Vergun, Dimitry *24-29*
Vetreria Corticella Felsinia srl. *100-103*

W

Walter, Robert *144-145*
Weiss, David *144-145*
Whitham, Bob *144-145*

PHOTOGRAPHERS

A

Ardiles-Arce, Jaime *94-97*
Aarons, Peter *114-117*

B

Berntsen, Tom *166*
Bonner, Tom *128-131*
Bourgeois, Nike *120-123*
Busher, Dick *89, 92-93*

C

Charles, Frederick *56*
Covey, Christopher *84-85*
Cunningham, Billy *30-31*

D

D'Antona, Edoardo *58-59*
Dow, Christopher *146-149*

F

Feinholz, Eitan *160-161*

G

Gottlieb, Jane *76-79*
Grapow, Janos *100-103*

H

Hall, John *113*
Hamer, Alec *32-35*
Hedrich-Blessing *104-105, 140-143*
Hill, Douglas *42-43*

J

Jensen, Michael *150-155*

K

Karicofe, Foster *40-41*

L

Lautman, Robert C. *14-17*
Livingston, David *164-165*

M

Miller, Jon *104-105*
Minton, Emily *162-163*
Mott, George *108-112*

N

Nichols, Mary E. *80-81, 106-107*

P

Peres, Anthony *74-75, 134-139*
Piazza, Matteo *62*
Piemonti, Giovanna *156-157*
Prohl, Undine *18-23*

R

Rand, Marvin *129*
Rosenberg, Al *126-127*

S

Santini, Claudio *21*
Sargent, Kim *64-67*
Shimer, Bob *140-143*
Shopenn, Michael Ian *88, 90-92*
Steinkamp/Ballogg, Chicago *60-61*
Street-Porter, Tim *82-83*

T

Tianen, Jussi *50-53*

V

von Schaewen, Deidi *118-119*

W

Warchol, Paul *54-55, 57, 68-73, 124-125,*
    166-171
Waugh, Richard *44-47*
Weintraub, Alan *24-29, 38-39, 144-145*

ACKNOWLEDGMENTS

Having benefited twice before from its high standards in the publication of *Empowered Spaces* (now released as *At Home & At Work*) and *Furniture: Architects' & Designers' Originals,* I am thrilled to have the opportunity to write four more books for PBC International, Inc. These four volumes were conceived as a series on the residential use of tile, stone & brick; wood; glass; and fabrics. Their development could not have been possible without the extraordinary commitment of Publisher Mark Serchuck and Managing Director Penny Sibal to good design. That Managing Editor Susan Kapsis has overseen and scrutinized their development fills me with a sense of security. Besides, with our interests being similar and our enthusiasm high, we have had a marvelous time!

PBC's Technical Director Richard Liu has again lent his expert analysis to make sure that only excellent photographic material prevails. And Garrett Schuh's design, sensitive to the subject, has kept me in a constant state of excitement. The art department's Barbara Ann Cast proved indispensable to the final execution of the layout. And to the editorial department's Dorene Evans, Donna Ahrens, Alyson Heegan and Sean Geist, for perfecting every detail—a million bouquets!

I was also most grateful to have had James Gabrie, Beatrix Jakots Barker and Tuula Stark come to my aid when I was desperately in need of translators, and to have had the admirably thorough Angeline Vogl proofread every word.

The list grows as I try to list the many people who have supported this endeavor as I have called their offices across the United States and throughout the world. Among those who have been especially helpful with this volume are Ake Danielson, Deputy Consul General of Sweden; Tatu Tuohikorpi, Deputy Consul General of Finland; and Mitchell P. Strohl, Strohl & Strohl Company, Inc.